Na

Naughty Girls' Night In

START YOUR OWN
SEX-TOY PARTY BUSINESS

(You Know It's Not the '50s
When You're Selling Your Girlfriends
Lingerie and Sex Toys Instead of Plasticware)

Shana Duthie and Stacey Jewell

Ulysses Press

Published by: Ulysses Press
　　　　　　　P.O. Box 3440
　　　　　　　Berkeley, CA 94703
　　　　　　　www.ulyssespress.com

Library of Congress Control Number: 2004108856
ISBN 1-56975-434-9

Printed in Canada by Transcontinental Printing

10 9 8 7 6 5 4 3 2 1

Editorial and Production: Ashley Chase, Lisa Lee, Claire Chun, Lily
　　Chou, James Meetze, Steven Schwartz, Leona Benten
Cover design: Jack Flahetry
Interior design: Sarah Levin
Index: Sayre Van Young

Distributed in the United States by Publishers Group West
and in Canada by Raincoast Books

Table of Contents

Preface

A pair of good friends, both married with kids, we didn't know much about sex toys or home parties until about five years ago when we started looking for new ways to spice up our marriages. Searching at our local lingerie stores for some fun toys to make things more interesting, we found ourselves shopping next to men who made us uncomfortable and hesitant to ask about "the toy that goes buzz" for fear of sounding ridiculous. Next we tried shopping on an Internet site that was supposed to cater to couples but turned out to be a porno abyss with naked breasts staring us right in the face at every stop…. At that moment we decided to create our own way for women to shop for sex toys and more. That's how Lady Bliss was born, a company committed to celebrating and enhancing women's sexuality by offering them a safe and enriching shopping experience.

Before Lady Bliss we each worked as consultants advising businesses on how to perform better—Stacey in marketing and consumer research, Shana in finance and business operations. We took what we had learned from helping other companies achieve their goals and applied it to our own vision for Lady Bliss. Starting with www.ladybliss.com on the Internet, our goal was to create something different from anything else in the marketplace. This meant going through a lengthy process of researching the right products, the right packaging and the right way to present the products: pornography-free and discreetly wrapped—yet ready for romance.

Once the website was off the ground, we took our passion for enhancing women's sexuality directly into their homes with sex-toy home parties—they're like Tupperware parties, only with sex toys instead of plastic containers. Today Lady Bliss home parties are held all over the country. Our Lady Bliss representative program empowers women who have the drive to own their own business with an easy way to follow their dream.

Now we'd like to inspire you to follow your own dream. From our experience with starting and running Lady Bliss Home Parties has grown this book explaining the ins and outs of starting your own sex-toy party company, becoming a party representative for an existing company, or just hosting a party at your own home. We give you advice on sales and marketing, the best products to carry, business structure, and more.

Our philosophy is and always will be to live a life that is full of "caring, sharing and being daring." Dare to take the leap into this daring new business. If we can do it so can you....

Good luck,
Stacey Jewell and Shana Duthie

PART ONE

Naughty Girl Parties for Nice Girls Who Want to Have Fun

So, you're asking, who are naughty girls and just what are these parties all about? Close your eyes and picture this....

A hip dance beat underscores the conversation as ten to fifteen gal pals kick back in a comfy living room. They're sipping drinks, nibbling munchies, and catching up on the gossip— who's got a new boyfriend, whose husband remembered their anniversary, who's planning a weekend escape. As you circulate among the crowd, you hear laughter and giggles. You also hear things like: "That little thing changed my life" and "What do you suppose you do with this?" The answer to that question will follow in an evening of rollicking sexy fun.

Sex-toy parties are a fabulously fun and discreet way for people to learn about erotic products and how to use them, both for romance and solo pleasures. In addition, these parties are a fun and lucrative business. As a hostess, you can earn credits, commissions or free gifts while giggling and talking about S-E-X with your best friends. As a representative of a home-party company, you can build a flexible part-time business that works around your busy lifestyle. You could also start your own independent home-party business, maybe even become a sex-toy tycoon. Sex-toy parties will have you beaming all the way to the bedroom—or the boardroom!

But before we give you all the juicy details on sex-toy parties, it's important to start at the beginning, when the home-party phenomenon was born....

ONE

It's Not Your Mom's Tupperware: The Home-Party Phenomenon

Does a burping container with a pink lid ring a bell? Tupperware is now an American institution, and it just happens to be the first company to start home parties in this country. In the 1940s, Tupperware was getting lost on the shelves of hardware stores and the company was going under. Thanks to the innovative ideas of a woman named Brownie Wise, these handy containers are now found in almost every home in America. Ms. Wise, inventor of "the Tupperware Party," revolutionized the kitchen and social lives of house-wives across America, advancing feminism in the process and earning Tupperware a place in everyone's kitchen. A life-time's worth of her documents is preserved in the archives of the Smithsonian Institution's Museum of American History.

So what did Brownie Wise do? She had the brilliant idea to take Tupperware into women's homes, where they were comfortable, and use women themselves as salespeople to demonstrate the products and share their personal experience and expertise. Her business model was revolutionary, too: working on commission only, a Tupperware distributor (or representative) would recruit an acquaintance to invite friends and neighbors to a party at her home. The distributor would take products that she bought directly from Tupperware and demonstrate the power of the Tupperware container "burp" to partygoers. At the end of the party, she would take orders from the partygoers. As a thank-you for providing her home and the customers, the hostess received free gifts. What a great system! Everyone had fun, and everyone profited—some personally, some professionally!

If not for Brownie Wise and her novel idea of demonstrating products in the convenient privacy of a customer's home, Tupperware would never have survived—and the home-party phenomenon may never have been born.

To give you a glimpse into how the Tupperware Party phenomenon has grown, consider these facts: Somewhere in the world a Tupperware Party begins every 2.5 seconds. Nine out of every ten American homes have at least one piece of Tupperware in their cupboards. Tupperware made over one billion dollars in sales in 2003, mainly by empowering 950,000 independent salespeople who demonstrated the beauty of airtight containers to the 105 million people who attended Tupperware parties. This is quite amazing for a company that was going broke fifty years ago.

Today the home-party phenomenon generates an estimated 130 billion dollars in sales, selling everything from candles to home décor, jewelry, makeup and cooking items. When
Ms. Wise burped her first container at the inaugural Tupperware Party in the 1950s, we doubt she realized she was starting a movement. The birth of the home-party industry has
provided women with a unique way to earn extra income
and work flexible hours while raising their children. This is
yet another reason why the home-party industry has increased
substantially over the last twenty years.

Are you thinking, "That's all well and good, but what
does this have to do with my love life?" Think about it: if plastic containers can make that kind of money, imagine what
erotic products can do. Racy home-party gatherings first
started in the early '70s, inspired by the sexual liberation movement. It was not until the late '80s and early '90s, however,
that sex-toy parties really caught on. With the arrival of HIV
and AIDS, sex—and our willingness to talk about it openly—
changed. As herpes and other sexually transmitted diseases
became featured daily in local newspapers, people weren't
spreading free love anymore, but they were talking about how
to make it safer and better. And they were talking about how
to make relationships stronger.

Inspired by the Tupperware party and the Avon Lady,
sex-toy companies realized they could introduce erotic products to women in the comfort of their own homes. Up to this
point, the sex-toy industry catered solely to men. Curious
women had to brave the local sex-toy store, where male customers peered at them, men worked the cash register, and

their next-door neighbor or minister might catch them going in or out. Not a friendly situation at all!

The women-oriented home party is now revolutionizing women's romantic lives. Today's sex-toy industry is more open, educational, sex-positive *and* lucrative than ever before. The sex-toy party industry is now estimated at a whopping 86 billion dollars per year worldwide. And it's growing—which means there is room for it to enhance your life, too!

In the chapters that follow, you will learn about the different ways you can get involved in this fun and exciting industry—whether you want to hostess a party, become a party representative who visits people homes or start your very own sex-toy party business. We have pulled together practical advice, dos and don'ts, business wisdom earned through our trials and errors, and fun and educational anecdotes from the Lady Bliss business, in hope that you will be inspired to take up the business and bring bliss to many women's lives!

TWO

Portrait of the Perfect Party

We've written this chapter to show you all the things that go into a great sex-toy party. One of the most important elements of a party is the hostess—and you'll notice that there's lots of advice for hostesses in this chapter. No, we haven't forgotten this is a book about starting your own business, but hostessing advice is valuable here for two reasons. First of all, hostessing is a good way to get your feet wet and learn more about this business before making a major financial commitment. Second, to be a successful rep you need to be able to communicate with your hostess and explain what her role is. (And unless you work for a company that provides hostess information packets, you may want to create an information packet yourself.)

A successful party is all about the collaboration between the hostess and the party representative, so we've written this chapter for the two of you—hostess and rep. Whichever role you're in, this chapter will tell you what you need to know to throw the perfect sex-toy party.

The Perfect Guests

Got your pad and pencil ready? It's time for the hostess to draw up a list of friends and acquaintances. When putting your guest list together, consider all the fun, open and adventurous women you know. Who is game for anything? Who is sexually curious? Who enjoys a night out with the gals? These women should be at the top of your list.

You should think twice about inviting your grandmother or great-aunt Edna—unless Aunt Edna reeeeeally likes S-E-X, and you're not uncomfortable talking with her about it. You also want to avoid any friend or work colleague who is mortified by the word "vibrator," or who would be embarrassed bumping into you at work on Monday morning. The best choice for guests are women you know personally who are open to new and exciting things that will enhance their sexual relationships.

WHAT'S A REP?

A rep, or representative, is a salesperson for a home-party company who demonstrates products at parties and takes orders. Whether you plan to work for an existing company or form your own small business, the rep advice is for you.

It might be fine in a restaurant, but a party of two won't be a success in this context. You'll need at least five guests to make the sales potential of the party worth the time investment. Many sex-toy party companies actually require a minimum of five or even ten guests, while others leave the number to the discretion of the rep. A few smaller companies and some individual reps require a deposit from the hostess that will be refunded from the party sales, to insure that the rep makes a minimum amount even if no guests make purchases.

To make sure you have enough guests, over invite! Inevitably some people will not be able to attend, and some will confirm but not show. Our advice is to invite *two to three times* the number of guests required, and encourage guests to bring friends. Inviting more people than you need ensures a successful party for both hostess and rep, because the more that is sold at your party the higher the rep's profits and the more incentives the hostess can earn.

The Perfect Occasion

Bachelorette and birthday parties are even more fun as sex-toy parties, but you don't need a special occasion to throw one. Ordinary weekend nights are often the best time to throw a party. That said, we have also had some very successful parties on weekend afternoons. Some reps say that Tuesdays and Thursdays are good days for parties, because those are nights when people tend to be free. Your timing really depends on what will work best for you and your friends.

Thinking of a having a party right before Valentine's Day, Christmas or New Year's so you can stock up before these romantic occasions? We recommend you avoid throwing parties during the holidays, since people travel and have busier social schedules then. At holiday time people are more hesitant to commit, and likelier to flake out, than at any other time of year.

The Perfect Invitation

Invitations are key because they form the guests' first impressions of a sex-toy party. They set the tone and get guests

TALES FROM LADY BLISS LIFE

When making up your guest list, think about who would enjoy a sex-toy party. We'll never forget the bachelorette party that a hostess threw for her mother, a very modest woman who had been married to a Mormon minister for twenty years and was getting ready to remarry a Catholic. The party was attended by mothers and daughters, and the generation gap between them soon became apparent. The older women's embarrassment during our presentation was nothing compared to their horror when the male stripper arrived. After taking off his uniform, this "fireman" really put out any fire left at the party. The poor guest of honor was subjected to his bumping, grinding and licking while her daughters egged him on (and we gathered up our products and hid)!

The generation gap can go both ways: We once served a party for a group of enthusiastic twenty-somethings. As the party was winding down, the hostess' mother came home. Upon spotting one of the more unusual dildos, she regaled the group with a story about the time her husband brought home the biggest dildo she'd ever seen, suggesting he poke her in the butt with it. The hostess was mortified, to say the least. So remember, your guest list is not only about who will enjoy the party, but who will help you enjoy it too.

excited and enthusiastic. Be sure your invitations make it clear that partygoers will be shown products at the party, and that the products have to do with sex. Here's an example from a Lady Bliss invitation to give you the idea: "You'll see exciting new products that are made to enhance the romance in your life. Whether you prefer beautiful erotic kits, the fun of an

adult toy or the sensuality of a tasty treat, you'll find everything you desire for a more fulfilling love life. Please come
join us and bring a friend to see what these exciting parties
are all about."

Reps, you can help your hostesses out here. Providing
invitations to hostesses is a great way to promote your parties.
Some reps even do the work of sending out the invitations
for their hostess. Lady Bliss offers an e-mail invitation service on our website; we also provide printed invitations for
our hostesses. We have found, however, that many hostesses
choose to send their own invitations, because they know their
friends and what to say.

We think the best way to invite people is for the hostess
to call them personally, then follow up with a written invitation. If your group of friends is wired, e-mail invitations—
such as Evites—can make your job easier. A neat feature of
Evites is that you can set a follow-up reminder to be auto-
matically mailed out a few days before the event to everyone
who RSVPs "yes." This may help ensure a better turnout.

The Perfect RSVP

The more time you give your guests to arrange their schedules, the better the chances that you will have a well-at-
tended party. Make your phone calls and send the invitations
to your guests at least one to two weeks in advance of the
party. Then, two to three days before the party follow up
with your guests to confirm their attendance. This also gives
you another chance to stir their excitement for the event.

The day before the party, the two of you—hostess and rep—should touch base. If you haven't had confirmation from a minimum number of guests, be prepared to reschedule.

What about those invitees who wish they could come to the party but have a prior engagement? If your party company has a catalog, the hostess should get plenty of copies to pass along to friends who can't make it to the party but might want to place an order. Any orders the hostess gathers before the party should count toward the party sales total. Hostesses, don't just hand someone a catalog and cross your fingers hoping she'll make an order. Drop off the catalog personally and take time to talk with your friend. Discuss some of the products that you find exciting or that you think she might like. Tell her about the reactions you expect at the party. Then commit to a time when you can pick up her order before the party. Reps, make sure you're available to the hostess' friends, whether they are able to attend the party or not, to answer any questions they may have about the products, ordering process or delivery. They're potential customers too.

The Perfect Refreshments

As my grandma always says, a well-fed party guest is a happy party guest! Hostesses, the next thing to do after perfecting your guest list and sending out all the invitations is to plan your menu. Remember, this is a party about making S-E-X more pleasurable and exciting, so providing food and drinks for your guests is a must for encouraging festivity and fun. Tasty nibbles and cocktails will warm up your guests for the big presentation.

If cooking is not your forte, you don't have to prepare an elaborate spread. You can pick up attractive finger foods from your local deli, grocery or club store. Hummus with pita bread, garlic and herb cheese with rice crackers, chips and dips, and fresh vegetables are all good munchies. Or why not pick up pre-made sandwiches from Subway or Quiznos? And don't forget dessert! Cookies, cupcakes and ready-made fruit salad are an easy indulgence. Combine any of these snacks with a bottle of wine (or two) and your party is ready to go.

On the other hand, if you love being in the kitchen, break out some of your favorite recipes. A few of ours are on page 14. If you're inspired, you can pair your food and wine in a sexy theme. You may also want to check out Lady Bliss' favorite cookbook, *Intercourses: An Aphrodisiac Cookbook* by our friend Martha Hopkins, which has recipes and drinks to get your libido in full gear. We always encourage our hostesses

TALES FROM LADY BLISS LIFE

You don't want your guests to overindulge. We did a party for a group of grade school teachers who got drunk and rowdy. We figured that they must have had a rough week and needed release because they partied like we had never seen before or since. We had to stop our presentation many times so as not to yell over them. And later we caught them sneaking the clitoral stimulation cream into the bathroom to try it out! We hid our shock— then we hid the vibrators because we were afraid they were next! The motto here? You must buy it to use it!

to experiment with their cuisine. Like sex, cooking is a fun and creative way to open your senses and express yourself!

If you are serving cocktails and your group is larger than five, consider making pitchers of drinks. They look attractive, and this way you can spend your time at the party being a hostess instead of a bartender.

In addition to wine, beer or cocktails, make sure to offer attractive non-alcoholic beverages. Some of your guests may be designated drivers or on a diet, or they may just prefer to abstain. And while alcohol is a wonderful "social lubricant" that can help the party get rolling, you want to avoid excessive or wild partying for strategic reasons. Drinking too much turns the emphasis away from the sexy educational focus of your party.

TASTY NAUGHTY GIRL PARTY RECIPES

YUMMY HOT ARTICHOKE DIP

    1 8-oz package cream cheese, softened
    1/2 cup sour cream
    1/2 cup mayonnaise
    2 cloves crushed, minced garlic (pre-minced garlic is sold
       in the produce section of most grocery stores)
    1 cup parmesan cheese
    1 can of artichoke hearts (not marinated)
        Preheat oven to 350 degrees. Blend all the ingredients (except for artichoke hearts) with a beater or spatula. Once all ingredients are well blended, drain and finely chop the artichoke hearts. Mix with the blended ingredients. Place in an ovenproof dish and bake until dip is hot and bubbly (about 20 minutes). Serve with crackers or pita chips…delicious!

COLD AND CREAMY VEGGIE PIZZA

This is an easy dish that you can prepare beforehand.

  1 package refrigerated crescent rolls
  1 8-oz package cream cheese, softened
  1 tsp mayonnaise
  1 clove garlic, finely minced (pre-minced garlic is sold in
     the produce section of most grocery stores)
  salt and pepper to taste
  2 cups of your favorite fresh vegetables, sliced (broccoli,
     cauliflower, onion, mushrooms, zucchini, spinach, red
     or green onion, bell pepper, carrot are all good)
  2 cups cheddar cheese, grated

Preheat oven to 350 degrees. Unroll crescent dough and separate the eight triangles. On a large pizza pan arrange triangles in a circle with points in the center. With a lightly floured roller, roll out the dough, pressing seams together to seal. Bake 12–15 minutes until light golden brown. Remove and cool completely.

In a bowl combine cream cheese, mayo, garlic, salt and pepper. Mix well with an electric beater or spatula. Spread the mixture evenly over the crust.

Sprinkle cut vegetables over the top of the pizza. Cover evenly with cheddar cheese and voila…a fabulous finger food!

LAYERED TACO DIP

This is fabulous served with a pitcher of margaritas!

  1 16-oz can refried beans
  1 8-oz package cream cheese, softened
  1 cup sour cream
  2 Tbsp taco seasoning mix

2 cloves garlic, finely minced (pre-minced garlic is sold in
the produce section of most grocery stores)
2 cups shredded cheddar cheese
1/2 cup sliced pitted olives
1 medium tomato, diced
1/4 cup green onion, diced
2 Tbsp fresh cilantro
As many tortilla chips as you like!

Preheat oven to 350 degrees. Spread refried
beans over the bottom of an oven-safe baking dish.
In a bowl combine cream cheese, taco seasoning mix,
sour cream and garlic. Mix well with an electric
beater or spatula. Spread cream cheese mixture evenly
over beans. Cover with shredded cheddar cheese.
Bake for 15-18 minutes or until hot.

After taking dip out of the oven garnish with
chopped tomatoes, olives, green onions and cilantro.
If you want to add more sour cream to the top for
good measure, go for it!

SEXY DRINK IDEAS

CHOCOLATE KISS MARTINI
1 part Frangelico
1 part vodka
1 part crème de cacao
1 chocolate Hershey's Kiss

SEX ON THE SOFA
2 parts vodka
1 part peach schnapps
2 parts orange juice
2 parts cranberry juice

SLOW COMFORTABLE SCREW AGAINST THE WALL WITH A KISS

> 2 parts vodka
>
> 2 parts sloe gin
>
> 2 parts Southern Comfort
>
> 1 part Galliano
>
> 1 part amaretto
>
> Top with orange juice.

The Perfect Setting

You'll need two rooms to hold a party: a larger party room for socializing and watching the presentation, and a smaller private room for taking individual orders after the presentation. Ideally, your party room should be big enough for everyone to sit comfortably and have a good view of the products. If your place is small and your crowd is casual, large throw pillows can create floor seating. As hostess you can help set the mood, according to your crowd. We've served parties with loud music and others with quiet music, some with bright lights and others with dim lights, candles and incense—you name it. Just make sure you turn the music off once the presentation starts, so that partygoers can focus on the main event.

If possible, clear off a table and place it in the front of the party room where your guests will gather. This is where the rep can display her items, giving your guests the opportunity to view the products before the party starts and ask any questions they may have. If you don't have a table, or don't have much room, work with what you do have. We've done presentations with fireplace mantles, small coffee tables, bookcases and even chairs as the display area.

Place food and drinks in a spot that is accessible, not tucked away in a corner. If your place is small, you can have food and drinks in the kitchen, where people can make up small plates to take into the party room. This will leave enough space for the presentation products in the party room. Set out your prepared food before your guests arrive so you can enjoy the party along with everyone else.

Now, Let's Party!

Have you heard the saying that success is 10 percent inspiration and 90 percent perspiration? Well, we say it's actually 90 percent *preparation*. Be prepared and you won't have to sweat the details! Hostesses, have everything prepared and in place at least a half hour before your guests are due to arrive. Reps, that's when you come in—always arrive early to set up. As the rep sets up the display table, the hostess should be watching and asking questions so you can share your excitement with the guests.

Finally, your guests start arriving and your rep smiles and starts to introduce herself to everyone. After everyone has arrived, let them mingle and socialize, sampling the food and sipping drinks. They will probably check out the display table on their own as well. Don't be surprised if the girls come in, get a drink and want to get started right away because they are so excited about the products. You don't have to wait until everyone has arrived to get started: latecomers are easily caught up in the festivities. When the two of you decide the time is right, the hostess should introduce the rep to the crowd and let her take center stage.

HOSTESS DOS AND DON'TS

- **Do** remind guests to be on time.
- **Do** have enough chairs and comfortable seating for guests.
- **Do** make sure you introduce yourself to everyone as they arrive.
- **Do** encourage conversation about the products, but don't drown out your party rep's presentation.
- **Do** have plenty of food and drinks for your guests.
- **Do** have a separate room available for the rep to take your guests' orders in private.
- **Do** interview reps so you match their personality (and product line) with your partygoers.
- **Don't** let your friends get so drunk that the party gets out of control.
- **Don't** forget to say "thanks for coming" when guests leave.
- **Do** protect people's privacy. **Don't** talk to friends about what partygoers ordered.
- Lastly, if you're having a stripper at the party, **do** the product presentation first and save the stripper for dessert! (And **don't** hire a stripper for your religious mother's bachelorette party.)

Break the Ice with a Little Spice

Reps, now it's your turn. We find the best way to begin is by sharing a little bit about yourself and your company, and then starting the festivities with a game to break the ice. Party games can be absolutely hilarious and get the girls in the right frame of mind to talk about sex, vibrators and tasty oral sex surprises. Make sure you bring some fun little products to give away as prizes—sample sizes of body products, tasty lubes or orgasm boosters, inexpensive dice games, anything appealing

HOSTESS TIPS:
PICKING A COMPANY

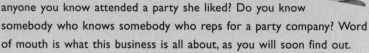

There are lots of party companies out there today to suit different tastes and attitudes. If you're planning to host a party, how do you determine which would be a good fit? An easy place to start is with your girlfriends. Has anyone you know attended a party she liked? Do you know somebody who knows somebody who reps for a party company? Word of mouth is what this business is all about, as you will soon find out.

If you don't have a strong personal recommendation, the Internet is a great resource. Just type "erotic home parties," "sex-toy parties," or "naughty girl parties" into any search engine and you will find websites for many party companies, including Lady Bliss, Passion Parties and others. Most of these websites have a hostess overview, which will give you a feel for the style and product selections of the company. They also have hostess applications that you can fill out online to signal your interest. If the company you choose is professional, someone will contact you shortly to answer your questions and make arrangements for your party.

All of the larger sex-toy party companies offer gifts or incentives to the hostess for providing the home and the customers. Typically, the hostess receives 10 percent off her order if the total party sales exceed a minimum of $300. Depending on the total sales at the party, the hostess will probably receive a free gift—the bigger the sales, the better the gift. Most party companies will also offer incentives for additional party bookings that come from the hostess' party (from $5 to $25, depending on the company). Check out "Hostess Rewards from the Major Party Companies" on page 26, which compares the benefits of hostessing for five popular party companies. We list the company websites and phone numbers, so this is a great place to begin your search.

Whether you are looking for something classy or racy, modest and couples-oriented or swinging and single, with a little bit of research you should be able to find a a nice fit.

that won't cut too far into your bottom line. A little marketing trick is to make small labels with your name, phone and e-mail or website address, then stick them on the prizes. Once the customer uses the sample up, assuming she liked it, she'll be able to come back to you for a future purchase.

Some games require pen and paper, so bring some along or ask your hostess to have them on hand.

Here are a few of our favorites:

Name That Body Part   This is a relatively simple game where guests are given two minutes to think of and write down as many slang words for the male anatomy that they can. When time is called, go around the circle and have each one read their list aloud. The person with the most names wins. This game is an easy way to get people laughing and talking about sex—and you will learn that a lot of penises have some unusual pet names!

Dream Lover   This game is best played when you have a group who know each other well. Each woman writes down the name of her dream lover on a slip of paper and then places it in a bowl. One by one, read each slip of paper aloud, as the party guests write down which person they think matches each dream lover. When all names have been read, go down the list and have each person confess to who their dream lover is. The person with the most correct matches wins.

Unscramble the Naughty Words   This game is simple but requires advance preparation. Create a list of naughty words – body parts, sexy terms, slang phrases—and then scramble the letters. Give each guest a sheet of paper with the scrambled words. Everyone has one minute to unscramble as many words as she can. Depending upon the word scrambling skills of your guests, you can end up with multiple winners, so be prepared with lots of gifts.

Dirty Dictionary   Make a list of naughty words and phrases again, choosing as many unusual and humorous terms as you can—"the man in the boat" (meaning "clitoris"), "pitching a tent" (meaning "erection"). Ask guests to write definitions for each term. When everyone is finished, read the correct answers aloud. Tell your party guests to circle the ones they got right. The guest with the most correct definitions is the winner. Invite willing party guests to read off their wrong answers after the correct ones have been read—it could inspire a big laugh.

Guess What's on the Platter   This is a great game to get the partygoers interested in your products. Using an inexpensive platter, place five to eight of your products on top. When everyone is sitting down, place the platter in the middle of the group. Give them a minute to examine what is on the platter and then take it away. Give the party guests two minutes to write down all of the products they saw on the platter and then have them read their lists. Whoever gets the most correct wins.

Just for fun, you might want to hand out consolation prizes for best wrong answer, etc. Once the girls are giggling and having a great time, they're ready for the presentation.

The Main Event

What would a sex-toy party be without sex toys? It's time for the presentation. Reps, now you show your products to the group, explain how each one works and tell everyone how the products can help make their sex lives terrific. The perfect presentation is educational *and* entertaining, interspersed with questions and banter. You are the expert— actually, the sexpert!—and should be able to respond to guests' questions, interests and concerns. We'll give you lots of advice on presentations and pitches in Chapter 4, so for now we'll just say that a good presentation includes useful information, humor, personal stories and hands-on participation from the guests. At the perfect party, the guests will be listening and smiling while they pass around all of the products, wanting to taste and touch everything.

The average presentation takes one to two hours. Break every so often to ask if people have any questions. The party guests need time to digest what they are learning, so taking breaks for questions, dessert or refilling people's drinks will give them a chance to ask questions and absorb what they've seen before you show the next wave of products. Give them the chance to ask questions privately afterward as well.

TALES FROM LADY BLISS LIFE

A good party rep will show you how toys work and explain all the great ways they can be used, but she won't actually simulate steamy action. We've heard from some customers who hold an annual "Naughty Couples Party" with us that the representative from another company they used previously blew them away—literally. During her presentation, the representative simulated a blowjob with a dildo, prompting the men to throw dollar bills at her—and the women to throw her out!

HOSTESS TIPS: CHOOSING A REP

Before inviting a party representative into your home, take time to interview your potential rep over the phone. Make sure that you feel comfortable with her. Will she put your guests at ease? Will she get them excited and inspired? Does she explain things well? You want someone who has experience and knows what it takes to make a party successful. The interview is also your opportunity to gather details from the rep on how she will run the party.

Questions you might want to ask include:

- What types of products will you be presenting? (*Make sure the products she describes are within your guests' comfort level.*)
- How do you present the products? Do you teach partygoers about the uses of the products? How do you keep the presentation fun? (*Get a feel for how well she knows her product line.*)
- Will you lead party games and give out prizes?
- How long does the presentation usually take?
- How will guests receive the items they purchase at the party? Will the products be available at the party itself? Will you mail each guest's order directly to her after the party? (*Find out whether you will have any responsibilities for delivering orders to guests after the party.*)
- Is there a fee for throwing the party? Will a minimum number of guests be required?
- How long have you been with the company?
- How will you help me prepare for the party so it can be successful?
- What kind of incentives or free gifts will I receive as a hostess?
- What incentives will I receive if one of my guests books a party?

If you are not satisfied with the answers to these questions, then this representative and possibly her company are not right for you. Since there are many companies (and even more reps!) to choose from, you should be able to find one that suits your interests and comfort level.

Reps, finish your presentation by letting party guests know that you'll be taking orders in another room to give everyone privacy. You might linger around the products for some time first, assisting guests who would like to take a second look, ask questions they may feel shy about or make a list of things they would like to buy.

Then invite guests to give you their orders one by one in the other room. Depending on whether you carry inventory, guests will place orders for shipment at a later date or receive their products on the spot. The order process for all the guests takes no more than an hour, and usually much less. When we do parties in pairs, one of us takes orders while the other assists partygoers at the display table, answering questions and helping them fill out order forms.

The Party's Over

After orders are taken, the rep will pack up, say her good-byes and depart…but this usually isn't the end of the party. Guests will stay on, laughing and partying, inevitably talking about the discoveries they've just made. Hostesses, when the party winds down, thank your guests for coming and wish them future fun with their new discoveries. Some hostesses like to pass out party favors, especially if their party is in honor of a bachelorette or a birthday girl, but this is not required.

When the party is done, the end result should be a good time, where everyone learned something new and exciting while feeling sexy, empowered and all the better for having attended.

HOSTESS REWARDS FROM
THE MAJOR PARTY COMPANIES

This chart shows what each of the major party companies covered in the book give as their hostess rewards. Remember that many reps offer their own gifts and other rewards that are not part of the company plan.

	SLUMBER PARTIES	PASSION PARTIES	FANTASY LADY	LADY BLISS
HOSTESS CREDIT	The hostess receives a free credit worth 10% of the party sales total, which she can use to buy additional products.	The hostess receives a free credit worth 10% of the party sales total, which she can use to buy additional products.	The hostess receives a free credit worth 10% of the party sales total, which she can use to buy additional products.	The hostess receives a free credit worth 10% of the party sales total, which she can use to buy additional products.
HOSTESS GIFTS	If the total party sales are over $200, the hostess receives a small gift plus 40% off any one item.	If the total party sales are over $300, the hostess can choose one of two gifts.	Gifts are up to the individual rep.	If the total party sales are over $300, the hostess can choose one of five gifts. Larger gifts are also available when party sales exceed $500, $750, and $1000.
ATTENDANCE REWARDS	If 15 or more guests attend the hostess receives 40% off one item of lingerie.	It is up to the individual rep to give special gifts to the hostess for party attendance.	It is up to the individual rep to give special gifts to the hostess for party attendance.	It is up to the individual rep to give special gifts to the hostess for party attendance.
CONTACT INFO	www.slumber parties.com 800-240-2546	www.passion parties.com 800-4-Passion	www.fantasy lady.com 800-844-3868	www.ladybliss.com 866-352-5477

PART TWO

Parties for Profit

By now you have some good ideas about how to run successful sex-toy parties. You are passionate about passion and the things that can create it. This section covers everything behind the scenes that will transform you into a fabulous saleswoman who serves up popular, high-sales parties.

But before we get to the sales, we have to talk about marketing. Why? Sales don't happen without marketing. You can't craft the perfect sales pitch until you know who your customers are, what they want and what your competitors are offering them. When you start doing sex-toy home parties, customers look to you as an expert on sex—a sexpert. We'll tell you how to keep up on current trends, find information on sex and health that will benefit (and hook!) your customers, keep track of the competition and, if you're a rep, get the support you need from your company.

Then it all comes down to sales. If you don't understand the intricacies of your own product line...if you don't feel comfortable selling these products...if you can't convey to the customer how sex toys will make her life richer...if your samples look like they've been used and abused...you'll never make it in this business. We'll show you how to get to know your products intimately, practice your party pitch, take loving care of your sales kit, mesmerize a rowdy (or yawning) crowd of partygoers and, last but not least, make the sale. We'll also help you learn to care for your customers, because excellent service will keep them coming back.

Even the best saleswoman in the world can't sell anything unless she has customers to listen to her pitch. Whether you're working independently or as a rep for an established company, remember: It's your business and it won't just grow like a weed in the sunshine. Growth takes hard work and constant self-promotion. We'll tell you all about how to get your name out there, get party bookings and build your business—through networking, advertising, or any means necessary.

We invite you to come on in and explore your marketing side. When you are done you will have more tools to build a strong business....

THREE

Become a Sexpert: Market & Product Research

The first step to establishing a successful sex-toy party business is *knowing your market*: who are your customers and what are their interests? If you don't have any idea who you're selling to, you'll never get your business off the ground.

Most sex-toy party consultants will tell you that their best customers are women between the ages of 30 and 60, who are married or in long-term relationships and are looking to spice up their love lives. In our experience, parties for these women are the most common requests. However, who you target with your business really comes down to who you are and the type of women with whom you personally associate. These women are your *demographic*.

Here is an easy way to determine your demographic. Think about your ten best friends. Are they...

- Single or married?
- Adventurous or conservative?
- In their 20s? 30s? 40s? 50s and up?
- Straight, gay or bisexual?

Next ask yourself these questions for your larger circle of acquaintances. Then apply these questions to the women you encounter in your community—your neighborhood, church, volunteer activities, children's playgroup and so forth.

If you're a married woman with children, you probably associate with other married women with children and will start your sex-toy party business booking parties through them. If you are single you may know more single women. So if you are a twenty-something surrounded by other sex-positive twenty-somethings, then guess who your customers will be? At Lady Bliss, one of our reps is a lesbian who caters to other gay and lesbian couples. And we have had lesbian customers who request a lesbian rep because they feel most comfortable with one. So as you can see, your "market" starts with who you are and who you know and develops from there.

Do Your Homework! (Don't Worry: It's Fun)

Knowing your market also entails keeping up on the current sexual issues and pop culture trends that affect women in your demographic. Your customers will look to you to be an expert on these matters. So always make sure you've got sexy bedtime reading! Books, magazines and websites are fabulous resources for burgeoning sexperts.

Read the magazines that cater to your market. If you're mainly serving parties for married women in their 30s and

RECOMMENDED READS

Check out these favorites to beef up your sexpert credentials, and to learn more about erotic products and their many uses.

- *Great Sex for Moms: Ten Steps to Nurturing Passion While Raising Kids* by Valerie Davis, M.D. Very helpful to you when presenting to moms.
- *Toygasms! The Insider's Guide to Sex Toys and Techniques* by Sadie Allison. All you ever wanted to know about sex toys—and more!
- *The Good Vibrations Guide to Sex* by Cathy Winks and Anne Semans. A comprehensive resource by those fabulous folks at Good Vibes.
- *101 Nights of Grrreat Sex* by Laura Corn. A wealth of ideas for romantic adventures, from fairly frisky to all-out wild.
- *The Wild Guide to Sex and Loving* by Siobhan Kelly. This book talks about everything from foreplay to role play, from tantric sex to sex toys. It's a must have for every couple looking to spice up their sex lives.
- *Tickle Your Fancy: A Woman's Guide to Self Pleasure* by Sadie Allison. This how-to-guide explains in detail everything from the basics of getting started with masturbation to more advanced tips and techniques for enhancing self pleasure.
- *The Clitourist* by Karen Salmansohn. This is a witty guide to one of the hottest spots on earth, which can also help you educate your party-goers on the best route to get there.

40s, check out *Redbook*. If you deal with a younger single crowd, then *Jane* and similar magazines will keep you hip. *Cosmo* is always a great read, as it has a strong focus on sexuality and hot sex trends.

Reading books on sexuality is an excellent way of educating and selling to women at your parties. Browse the shelves at your local bookstore or read about new titles at Amazon. com (you'll find them under the "Health, Body & Mind" subject area). Currently tantric sex and the Kama Sutra are a popular and well-publicized trend with couples. A quick trip to your local bookstore will reveal that the shelves are stocked with books such as *Tantric Sex* by Nitya Lacroix, *Red-Hot Sex the Kama Sutra Way* by Richard Emerson, *The Tantric Art of Love* by Ray Stubbs, Ph.D, *Erotic Massage: The Tantric Touch of Love*, by Ray Stubbs Ph.D and Louis Andre Saulnier, and more—all good resources for you to read.

Keep in touch with television and radio shows dedicated to sexy trends and sexual information, such as HBO's "Real Sex," Oxygen's "Talk Sex with Sue Johanson" and "The Berman & Berman Show" and "Straight Talk About Men & Women's Sexuality" on the Discover Channel. Not only are they fun and educational, but these are the shows your customers might be watching. If their audience is representative of your customer base, they also cover topics that will be of concern to your customers. And they are perfect to watch on those nights when you just want to chill out! Just think, you can enjoy them all in the name of business research!

This fun "research" will help you stay in tune with your customers, assist you in making sales, and keep you (and your customers) up to date on any new products and trends dealing with sexuality. Reading and watching everything you can about sex will also help you become more comfortable selling erotic products. This may sound strange: why would you sell sex toys if they make you uncomfortable? There is a big difference between shopping for toys at a party and becoming a coach and counselor for women on their sexual experiences.

When you're in the business, you need to be comfortable explaining sexual details, listening to others' intimate concerns, and answering questions without embarrassment.

Take It to the Streets

To stay truly informed about current trends, you can't just do research at home alone—you have to take it to the streets. Get out there and talk to people, and see for yourself what's out there. Here are some ideas to help you get started.

KEEP ABREAST OF NEW PRODUCTS

We have been known to lament, "so many products, so little time…!"Just as you need to keep tabs on the interests and trends of your target market, you need to be familiar with the products that will make them happy and know when new toys enter the market.

If you are a representative for an established sex-toy party company, stay in close contact with your "up-line"—the person (or people) who recruited you to join the company and trained you to be a rep. Your up-line should keep you updated on all new products that the company adds to their catalog, but don't wait to hear from them. Every company has different ways of keeping their reps informed of new products, from newsletters, local meetings or simply through their territory managers. Make sure you ask your up-line the best way of finding out about new products to add to your kit so you can keep your product line fresh and add new sales potential. Don't be afraid to ask for help. The people who brought you in should be able to answer your questions, and if they can't for some reason, they'll direct you to someone who can.

TALES FROM LADY BLISS LIFE

When we attended our first sex-toy trade show, we were extremely nervous. We weren't really sure what to expect, but we knew we had to learn about everything that was out there. While browsing the aisles, we walked into the booth of a company called American Latex. They had a massive display of vibrators and dildos—and all the salespeople were men. Not used to looking at this type of product in my everyday life, I was slightly embarrassed. As I was glancing over the display, a man's voice from behind said "Feel this!" as something I felt sure was a penis was slung into my hand. I jumped up, looked down and discovered a "looks and feels real" dildo in my hand. It felt so much like the real thing it is now a popular Lady Bliss offering.

CHECK OUT STOREFRONTS

Visiting your local lingerie-and-toy shop is another helpful way to keep up on trends and products that are selling in your marketplace. If something is new and trendy these shops will be sure to carry them, as they are regularly visited by sales-people and usually have a strong customer base they have built along the way. Retailers such as Good Vibrations, A Touch of Romance, Toys in Babeland, Lotions & Lace, and others have built businesses that cater to women and their tastes. They are classy, well-lit boutiques where you will likely find more women shopping than if you were to brave the novelty adult bookstore in the alley.

How do you work a retail store? As a potential customer and an information gatherer. Spend time browsing in these shops. What is the first thing that catches your eye when you walk in? Which products are in the prime sales positions: on display tables, at eye level, near the cash register? Pretend to be a customer and ask the clerk for recommendations. Salespeople usually know their products and their market well. Observe what women are buying and listen to the questions they ask the salespeople. All this will help you establish a deeper understanding of women's tastes and assist you in asking the right questions at your parties.

TALK WITH YOUR GIRLFRIENDS

Want the straight scoop? Talk to your friends!

Ask which types of products they are most curious about, which they are likely to buy, which they currently use. Take your product catalogs over to their place and go through them together. You may be pleasantly surprised at the knowledge your friends may have about erotic products, and as you know, women have definite ideas on what they like and dislike in bed. Make sure you get a variety of opinions. Speak with your sexually outgoing friends as well as those that are more conservative. Also talk to men if you are comfortable. They will also have advice on what they would like to see introduced into their bedroom, and you can share this information with your women customers. By communicating with your potential customers, you will get a diversity of opinions that will help provide you with enough information to choose a product mix that covers everyone's comfort level, and products you will feel confident and proud to be selling.

CHECK OUT ADULT NOVELTY AND SEX-TOY PARTY WEBSITES

Not all sex-toy party companies will show the products included in their kits on their websites because they may be afraid of giving away trade secrets, but some do. For instance, Fantasy Lady "Fun Parties" list the products in each kit they offer, but show no images. Lady Bliss Home Parties gives enough information to pique your interest but you must contact them if you want further information, as with Passion Parties. Not only does this help sex-toy party companies change their kits if an item is discontinued or not selling, it also helps ensure that their top-selling reps have an opportunity to grow their business by contacting those people who are interested in starting a sex-toy party business. However, if you find a company that shows products on their website this is a good way to research the right company for you or to find a good product mix if you are starting your own company. You can also check out websites of companies that are specifically geared to women—such as Good Vibrations at www.goodvibes.com, Toys in Babeland at www.babeland.com and Lady Bliss at www.LadyBliss.com. On these sites you can explore products that are meant for women, gather helpful sales advice and find health information that you can share with your partygoers if the need arises. These sites will also help you explore the industry as a whole, especially if you're not comfortable going into an adult novelty shop or do not want to deal with pornography.

Get a Leg Up from the Competition

Finally, one of the best places to get marketing and product information is from your competitors. Who are their customers? Who are they targeting with their promotional materials? How do their businesses work? You should always know what they are doing so you have a better idea of what makes you different from them.

If you are thinking about starting your own independent business, you may wish to hostess several different parties for your potential competitors, so you can see how they and their reps work. You might want to show some interest in working for their company as a representative and ask to accompany one of their reps to a few of her parties. If you are paired with a rep, try to gather as much information as possible. This will help you understand more completely what you are getting yourself into in the sex-toy party industry. (You can check out pages 94–97 for a comparison of different sex-toy party companies).

Some questions to ask are:

- Why did you choose the company you're representing over the others?
- Do the products in your kit sell well for you? Which sell best?
- Does one demographic buy more items than another?
- Do you get repeat business and bookings?
- Who usually attends your parties? (Age range, marital status, etc.)
- How much does the average guest spend?
- What, in your opinion, constitutes a successful party?
- What are your average party sales?
- How long does an average party last?
- What do you have to do to book parties? Do you place ads? Does the company you work for support you in marketing your parties?
- Do you ever get returns? How does your company handle them?

- How do you deliver products to your customers? Do they seem happy with that system?
- What happens to an unhappy customer?
- Is there a system in place for you to receive repeat orders?
- Does the company you work for compete with its representatives by also selling products through a website, storefront or other means?

The answers to these questions should give you a clearer understanding of what the women in your market will expect from you and how to serve them well so your business can be a big success.

FOUR

The Ins & Outs of Selling Erotic Products: Becoming a Professional Salesperson

In the sex-toy party business, you have to remember that you are not just selling erotic products—you are also selling yourself. No, we're not suggesting you take up the oldest profession: we mean that the experience of learning from you, joking with you and getting to know you will be an important part of the package for your customers. You need to be comfortable with people and crowds, and know how to control them if they are noisy or seem uninterested. It's important to know how to give a strong and educational presentation without being boring. You need to be able to share your own personal experiences, because this helps your guests relate to you and feel comfortable enough to confide in you and ask questions. You must also be sensitive enough to judge your audience and talk about sexuality in a way that won't sound vulgar to them, as that will turn people off to you and the products.

When you start selling erotic products you really have a lot of responsibility. Yes, it's a fun and wonderful way to make money, but now you have to keep in mind that people are now going to look at you as a "sexpert" of sorts, and that means you'd better know your products. You need to know how all of your products work and rehearse your presentation until you have it down to the last detail. If you don't know your products, or are not comfortable with them, your party guests will know it and you'll get a bad reputation. It's also important to take care of your products. Think about it: you're selling erotic products that go on sensitive areas of the body. What will it look like if you take out your products and things look dirty? Gross! And your sales will reflect it!

And most importantly, you have to look at the big picture of your business and not just be in it for the sale right now. You want to establish long-lasting relationships with your customers so they will want to come back for more, because it is easier to build on your existing business than trying to find new customers and parties all the time. That means you need to provide unbeatable customer service to your clientele and be approachable and accessible to them whenever they need you. Selling sex toys is extremely rewarding, because with each sale you know you're making someone's sex life a little better by encouraging her to try new things and explore her sexuality. Keep in mind that you are not only selling sex toys but also sexual fulfillment, which can include self-respect, erotic knowledge, romance and sexual fantasies.

Getting Up Close and Personal with Your Party Kit

To really get to know your products, you need to get up close and personal. Empty your party kit, spreading all of the products on the floor around you. Check them out and then place them in groups that make sense to you. For example, put all of your vibrators and dildos together, place the couple toys together, move tasty lubes and edible treats together...you get the picture. Then go through each group of products and examine each one. Check out textures, looks, vibrations, speeds, tastes and smells—all the attributes that make one toy different from another.

TALES FROM LADY BLISS LIFE

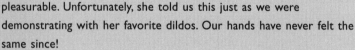

Please buy and keep separate the products you test drive—don't use them in your kit. This may sound like a no-brainer, but once when training a party rep, we learned that she'd taken everything in her kit for a spin, and found some of the toys very pleasurable. Unfortunately, she told us this just as we were demonstrating with her favorite dildos. Our hands have never felt the same since!

At Lady Bliss we have a favorite toy, the Bunny Pearl, that we give all Lady Bliss ladies as a special little gift. We call it the 30-second orgasm: long ears tickle your fancy and vibrating pearls pump up your pleasure. Whenever we describe the ecstasy that this little bunny can bring, our partygoers get wide-eyed over the possibilities. Let's just say, we sell lots of Bunny Pearls!

Put batteries in the toys that require them, and turn them on so you can feel the intensity of the vibration and all of the moving parts. Does a vibrator have three speeds? Check them all out! Hold it in your hand, then place it on your forearm or in the crook of your elbow, so that you can see how the same vibration feels in different or more sensitive parts of your body.

Got sexy couples games in your kit? Take all the game pieces out and read the instructions. Learn how to play the game so you can easily explain it to your customers. Open your warming lotions and rub them on the top of your hand so you can feel the warmth and know the taste—and imagine how it will feel on all of your erogenous zones. Rub, blow and lick these lotions until you experience their full range of sensation.

Knowing how your products taste, feel and work will give you a better idea for how to educate the women at your parties. Proper education means they will get the most satisfaction from the products they buy. And satisfied customers usually mean repeat business and referrals.

When you first purchase your party kit, we encourage you to buy extra goodies for yourself, so that have first-hand experience with the products. You might not be able to use them all before your first party, but you'll certainly have fun trying! At Lady Bliss we are big believers in test drives and personal recommendations. If you've never used any of the fun stuff in your kit with your own partner or to pleasure yourself, you cannot fully convey just how wonderfully these erotic products enhance women's and couples' sex lives.

Caring for Your Party Kit

Whether you buy your party kit from an established company or put together your own, you will have to decide how to cart your kit from one party to another. We have seen some reps carry their products in brown boxes, which in our opinion looks tacky and unprofessional. We recommend that our reps get suitcases with rollers to store their products in and take to each party. They don't need to be expensive, just nice enough to give your business a professional look, while showing the customers at your parties that you care for your products. We even have some highly organized reps who categorize their products according to how they're displayed and store each category of products in a separate plastic container.

You don't have to reach that level of organization, but we suggest that you arrange your case with the body products in one bag and everything else in a different bag (or bags). Body products can leak once they are opened, and you don't want them to spill on your toys, lingerie and other fun treats. This kind of organization also makes your unpacking smoother and quicker: when setting up your presentation table, you know where your products are and they are already properly grouped.

When packing up at the end of a party, make sure your toys are clean and everything is intact as you place the products back into their cases. You can buy individual wipes for your toys for convenience. If you cannot take care of cleaning right then, make sure to do so when you get home, so that everything is maintained and looks great for your next party. Remember, if your products don't look clean and well maintained, your business will look unprofessional and this will hurt sales. This may seem like a no-brainer, but you would be amazed at the product presentation disasters we have seen.

One last thing: don't store your kit in the trunk of your hot or freezing car, your garage or a separate storage area. Products need to be kept in a cool dry place, ideally in a closet or extra room in your house. This way nothing melts, your toys don't start to break down from excessive heat, things don't explode and you won't have to replace products.

Getting to Know Your Hostess and Her Guests

We always recommend to Lady Bliss home party reps that before they do any party they have a clear understanding of what their hostess wants presented. Most of the time, women love to see a wide variety of products—not only sex toys, but body products and romantic games as well. Sometimes your hostess may be shocked at what some of her friends seem most interested in. This actually makes the party a bit more entertaining, as the giggles are louder and more frequent. Be aware that every once in a while you will find a hostess who is a little dubious of the sex toys and wants the focus of her party to be on other products. But make sure you have the sex toys with you, as undoubtedly someone will have some interest.

Questions you might want to ask your hostess about her guests so that you will be well prepared:

- What games do you think your guests would like to play before the presentation? (You'll find directions for some fun party games in Chapter 2. Give your hostess a selection of at least three. Her choice will give you a better idea of how open your hostess and her guests are.)

- What products are you most interested in seeing? Which do you think your guests will want to see?
- Do your friends feel comfortable talking openly about sexual matters with one another, or are they more conservative?
- Are most of your friends married, divorced, never married, re-married or single?
- Do any of your friends have experience with erotic products that you know of?
- Have you ever been to a home sex-toy party before? Do you know anyone who has? What was the experience like?
- How many guests do you anticipate having?
- How well do the guests know each other? Are any of them coworkers?

All of these questions will help you gauge your party presentation properly so you can better fit the needs of the women who attend. What makes this business especially fun is that not every party is the same. As the needs of your hostesses change, your product presentation will have to be adjusted accordingly.

Practice Makes Perfect: Getting Your Party Pitch Down

Every great performance needs a dress rehearsal. To do a successful party, you'll need to feel comfortable—and knowing your pitch pitch-perfect is the best way to minimize stage fright. First, set up your table at home and arrange your products in different groupings to see which make the most sense to you. You can also try setting the products up on different tables to find ways they will display best at different hostesses' homes.

At our parties we like to set up the products into groups: romance toys and games, sex toys (dildos, vibrators, and couples toys) and unflavored lubes, tasty treats (flavored lubes, powders, warming oils and lotions), and body and massage products. This type of display helps to keep the presentation flowing, and if your guests are not familiar with the products, it makes things less confusing.

So with all these categories, what is the best place to start your pitch? After years of conducting parties, we have found that sex toys are the best opener. They get the presen-

---

TALES FROM LADY BLISS LIFE

Couples toys are always a big hit at parties, and later, in the bedroom. We recently received a letter from a customer who was certain that the new Mercedes her husband gave her for Christmas was a thank-you for the vibrating cock ring she had recently given him.

Once at a party we met the husband of a repeat customer. He thanked us for selling his wife a special couples toy—the Vibrating Silicone Cock Ring, which is one of our favorites, and had quickly become one of theirs. He said it had been a long time since he had seen his wife's eyes roll back in her head with ecstasy. Now that's a good feeling! And it's one of the reasons why we keep doing what we do.

tation off to a rollicking start. Women have more curiosity about these products than any other. These products definitely get the giggles going, and although we may not get a lot of questions during the presentation, women will often come up afterwards to us ask lots of questions and request help in deciding which products to choose for themselves. Other party reps have found that with shy or conservative groups, starting with romance products or lingerie is an effective way to ease the crowd into the racier items. It all depends on the nature of your partygoers.

To practice your pitch, talk to yourself: work out what you'll say about each product. Make sure you can describe how it works, and think of reasons why it's a must-have. Humor and personal experiences always help liven up a sales pitch. At Lady Bliss parties, we like to be interactive. We get people involved hands-on. We ask questions, tell funny stories, turn on the toys, pass them around. We encourage people to sniff, smell, smooth on and taste the different body products. We talk about toys' different uses and how women can incorporate them into their bedrooms for use with their lovers or to pleasure themselves. We also talk about proper toy care, so their sex lives can be happy and healthy. It is such fun to watch the different reactions that women have when they hold a vibrator or dildo in their hands for the very first time. Some hold it for a time, really experiencing the vibration and getting a feel for the product. Others are so intimidated that they pass it on like a hot potato. Many guests will be able to try new tastes and sensations that they may never have experienced before, so be prepared for excitement, embarrassment and a whole range of reactions. Practice pitching and demonstrating products in front of a mirror. Watch to see how you can best hold toys in such a way that an audience can see them.

When you feel ready, throw a practice party for your friends and family. Have them act as customers, asking you questions, making jokes and going through the order process with you. Afterward, ask them to give you constructive feedback on what worked for them and areas they think you can improve. (And then ask them if they want to place an order—you might be surprised at how many do!)

In the end, there's no better way to become an experienced party rep than to jump right in and present at a party. So pursue the first booking you get, go in with enthusiasm and an open mind, and just do it!

TIPS FOR SUCCESSFUL PARTY PRESENTATIONS

- **Don't be crude and rude.** No matter who your audience is or how they react to your products, be classy. You are a professional and your words and gestures should reflect that. Ultimately, nothing sells better than class.
- **Talk about your experiences.** If you have favorite products, don't hesitate to say so—and then explain why. Women want to know what really works for other women they can identify with.
- **Be enthusiastic.** Nothing sells like honest-to-goodness excitement. If you're passionate about these products (and you should be), let that passion shine through!
- **Be playful as well as educational.** This isn't biology class. Yes, there are women at most parties who really do want an anatomy lesson (and you should be prepared to give one)

TANTALIZING TEASING

Imagine…You blindfold your lover and instruct him to put his hands behind his back…no touching! You are the only one who can touch now. You take out your Hot Licks in Champagne and put it on his nipples. You blow on it to make it hot and start to lick, 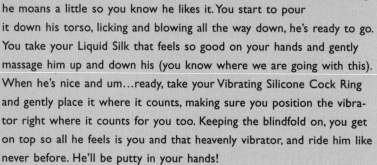 he moans a little so you know he likes it. You start to pour it down his torso, licking and blowing all the way down, he's ready to go. You take your Liquid Silk that feels so good on your hands and gently massage him up and down his (you know where we are going with this). When he's nice and um…ready, take your Vibrating Silicone Cock Ring and gently place it where it counts, making sure you position the vibrator right where it counts for you too. Keeping the blindfold on, you get on top so all he feels is you and that heavenly vibrator, and ride him like never before. He'll be putty in your hands!

but they're also there to have fun. So don't be afraid to laugh and make jokes with the crowd.

- **Sell the benefits, not the products.** We have a favorite vibrator, the Bunny Pearl, that we refer to as "the 30-Second Orgasm." It's not only one of our personal favorites, but it's one of our bestsellers. After all, who doesn't want a 30-second orgasm!

- **Stimulate their imaginations.** Don't just display a romantic product and show that it works. Explain how these sexy things can figure into a woman's love life. Paint pictures of romantic scenarios in which the products are used. Describe fantasies and how these products make them real. Help encourage the partygoers' desires. Our favorite opener is, "Imagine this…." When you become a rep it is your job to help evoke your party-goer's imagination for all of the different products you sell.

- **Don't be afraid to take a break.** Is someone looking confused? Is your audience beginning to glaze over? Take a short break to stretch your legs or get dessert. Refueling with food and drink gives your audience time to absorb everything they've seen and get refreshed for your next goodies.

- **Don't be discouraged by a shy crowd.** In our experience, shyness can actually mean larger sales. If your crowd is being quiet, maintain your enthusiasm, be gentle, and be prepared to talk a lot more during your presentation.

- **Let them taste, touch and feel.** Having women actually experience how wonderful something can be is the sure-fire way many of these sell. So tickle women's faces with feather dusters. Run massage toys along their backs so they know firsthand how good these feel. Encourage them to taste edible lubes, body creams and lickable powders. Let them smooth on and smell the lotions and massage oils.

- **If someone asks a personal question, try to answer it right away.** Inevitably, people will have questions during your presentation. Don't worry about being interrupted. Answering someone's question in the middle of your presentation gives you a better chance of selling the product, both to her and to the other partygoers. Provide your customers with plenty of opportunities to talk with you, including after the presentation in private.

- **Always ask if people have questions.** Just because no one has asked doesn't mean people aren't curious. They may be waiting for someone else to break the ice. Questions are an opportunity to make personal connections.

- **Be available outside the party**. Reassure the group that you are available outside the party as well. If you don't know the answer to someone's question, offer to do some research and get back to them. This is the customer service you need to provide to grow your business.

- **Say "thank you."** Send a thank-you note to the hostess, expressing your appreciation for the opportunity to serve her party. This letter is also a chance for you to give her a closing summary of the party: how many total sales were made, the hostess commission or thank-you gifts she's earned, whether any additional bookings came out of her party and whether she'll receive something for those bookings. Lastly, make sure to say thank you for the work that she put into the party to make it successful.

Mistress of Ceremonies: Mastering Crowd Control

Not every party is going to go as planned, and let's face it—that's life. We can't tell you how many times we have dealt with rowdy drunken women we had to scream over, as well as women who sat there, not saying a thing and just looking at us. It can be a little unnerving, but it's just part of the business. You want people to loosen up a bit and have drinks, but there's always that party where the girls just go overboard or remain quiet. Part of the party business, whether you are on your own or a rep for an established company, is finding a way that is comfortable for you to get some control over your crowd. Your hostess needs to be part of the solution as well. If things get out of hand she should help establish some control by talking to her friends and supporting you. However, you need to establish that with her from the beginning: don't just expect her to step up if you have not let her in on her responsibilities. Remember, she stands to gain from the party too—so if she has uninterested or rowdy partygoers who are not interested in buying, she loses out. With experience, mastering the crowd will come more naturally. But here are some tips to get you started.

When a party is large or the guests are loud and rowdy, you need to be aggressive to maintain control. Instead of trying to shout above them, grab their attention by getting them involved directly. Use some of the women to help demonstrate the products and don't be afraid to tell the crowd to be quiet. It will almost always work. If you have a crowd that is out of control, our advice is to stop talking. One of our favorite things to do is stick up two fingers, like an elementary school teacher giving the signal for quiet. It's funny—many of the women have seen this gesture before and understand that it means they are being an unruly "class," and that gets their attention. Once you stop they will usually notice and wonder why. That's when you ask them if they are interested in seeing more. If they are, ask them nicely to let you finish so they can enjoy the full experience. If they continue to act that way, just sit back, let your hostess know that it's worthless for you to continue trying and let her take a stab at controlling her crowd.

If you have a crowd of women who just look at you, don't really want to play your games and look like they are not having a good time, our advice is to keep on going. We have had these parties before, and they are almost worse than the unruly ones because while you are doing your best to present the products and be your witty, wonderful self, these women don't seem to agree that you and your products are wonderful. But never fear, things can change! Sometimes it just takes some time for these girls to warm up. We have found that they may be a bit more shy or really don't know one another, so being at one of these parties together can be a little embarrassing. With this type of crowd, you need to find a way to get them talking. You may need to play more games, encourage them to talk about themselves and also look for a common thread between the women. Most women will open up eventually, so be patient and continue to show your enthusiasm about the products. If you can get just one of the girls excited about a product, that may be all it takes to make everyone else feel at ease. Sometimes at parties like this, we've thought that our sales were going to be in the toilet but they ended up being huge. These guests tend to share their questions privately, during the time you take their order. They just need to be reassured that everything is confidential. You have to keep going and have faith, even when it seems there is none.

Making the Sale

After the presentation, you'll invite guests to place their orders privately and individually in a separate room. Your best bet is to try to sell a sex toy, along with a tasty lube. The bottom line is that sex toys make you the most money: they cost more, so your profits go up. The toys are what most of the girls will be curious about because, let's face it: these are not products you see everyday. However, you have to be sensitive to the fact that not all of the women who attend your parties will be comfortable buying a sex toy. This is why you need to be able to sell to a cross section of different personality types. If a customer doesn't feel comfortable buying a toy, you could sell a massage product with a massage oil and maybe a tasty treat.

You have to remember that many of the customers you encounter at your parties have had limited experience with sex toys and erotic products, so they will be looking to you for help. That's why it is so important to make each girl feel comfortable during the checkout period. Ask questions to make sure her erotic needs are being met. It's important to focus on the needs of the person you're selling to, keeping your bottom line in the back of your mind.

Depending on whether you're independent or a rep for an established company, and on which company you rep for, you may carry inventory to the party or process orders that either you or your company will ship out later. In Part Three you'll find lots of information on these issues of order fulfillment.

Caring for Your Customers

Do you remember the last time that you had a great sales experience? What about the last time that you had a horrible sales experience? We bet that you remembered the bad one right away and had to think about the good one: human nature is that we tend to remember our bad experiences. With that in mind, we believe that you need to treat your customers the way you would like to be treated—that if you had a complaint, you'd want someone to listen to it and find some sort of solution for you. Could that mean replacing the item that didn't satisfy you with another? Could it mean simply giving a refund with an apology for any inconvenience that may have been caused? Yes to all of that.

We find more and more in our society that customer service has gone out the window, especially in an age when we rely on computers—there's no one to talk to anymore! You simply cannot have that kind of policy in this type of business, one that is so personal and deals with customers' romantic needs. You will never have a successful business that lasts without paying attention and listening to your customers. We hope that the following information will give you the tools you need to better serve your customer base so you can build a successful business, in whatever terms that means to you.

THINK OF THE LONG-TERM RELATIONSHIP OVER THE IMMEDIATE SALE

If a customer is happy, she will return to you for future sales. Our reps get an average of at least one party booking from each party that they do. We always say, "Think about how you would want to be treated, that's how you need to treat your customers." You have to think about the big picture and that means not just doing the party as though this will be the last time you see these girls. Do the party as if these are going to become long-term customers. That's why being prepared, open, approachable and committed to customer service is so important, because that conveys how professional you are, how much you care about them and your business. If a customer is unhappy, she not only won't return, but most likely will tell others about her unhappiness. Think of yourself as the Nordstrom of erotic products—customer care is Nordstrom's trademark and it has been the key to their success. Show your customers how much you care about their business.

MAKE REPEAT SALES YOUR GOAL

Gaining a new customer takes three to four times as much work as getting repeat sales from current customers. Why is that, you ask? Because you have to constantly promote your business to get new parties and leads, which means some sort of marketing cost either in time or dollars. It is much cheaper to build on your existing customer than always having to go out and find new business. We are not saying that you should not be promoting your business and building it on an ongoing basis; you should be at all times. But your existing customers are the people who will have parties for you, buy from you and not someone else—and recommend you to their friends.

You have to think of it this way: when you're first building your business you are constantly having to convince your new customer base that you are different than everyone else, you have better products and are the person they should come to for romance products and sex-toy parties. At the beginning it's always toughest, of course, because you have not proven yourself to them yet. However, once your customers find that you are all of these things and more, while providing a safe and pleasant place to shop where they feel like they are number one and receive excellent customer service, why would they shop anywhere else? You need to keep in contact with past hostesses to let them know you are still around, let them know you appreciate them and their business, tell them about any new products you may be carrying, let them know about any new promotions you may be offering if they book another party, etc. The best way to do this is by calling, mailing flyers or doing a monthly newsletter. The bottom line is that happy customers make good recommendations, which means they will also help you acquire new customers and build your business.

BUILD POSITIVE WORD OF MOUTH

Negative word of mouth spreads much more quickly than positive word of mouth. We know how girls talk, especially about a sex-toy party they just attended. If they had a bad experience, and the rep doing the party was not professional or did not know her products (or the company that she was representing did not deliver products on time or had a terrible return policy), what do you think the odds are that the rep would get any other booking from that party? None. And the women attending would surely not recommend the products or the company to their friends. We have received more bookings than we can count from women who had bad experiences with other party companies because the orders were wrong, or the products didn't arrive in a timely manner, or the customer service was bad—the list goes on. We know from experience that if you don't deliver and take care of your customers the first time around, you might as well kiss them good-bye.

TURN COMPLAINTS INTO OPPORTUNITIES FOR CUSTOMER CARE

Basically, as a rep it is your responsibility to know your company's return policy and it should be part of the company's overall training as well. However, if it is not, it is still your

NERVOUS NELLIE

We got a call to do a party for someone who had thrown a home sex-toy party the previous year. The hostess did not re-book with the same rep because she had read her whole presentation from index cards, felt so nervous that she could not look at the crowd, was noticeably uncomfortable with the products and was not well trained. Needless to say, the partygoers were not impressed, and we are pretty sure the rep was discouraged by her experience. That is why we stress that you have to know your products, give a practiced presentation, be enthusiastic and prepare to do a knock-out show! Though it is your sex-toy party company's responsibility to help train you, it is your responsibility to have your presentation down to the last detail. Because if you're not ready, your customers will know it, and probably will never book a party with you again, let alone order any more products from you. The bottom line is this, you are selling not only sex toys but yourself, whether you are with an established sex-toy party company or are on your own.

job to take care of your customers, as it is ultimately your business and you have a chance to make an unhappy customer into a lifelong customer by the way you handle their complaint. If you are repping for a company it should be a team effort, working together to resolve the issue, and if you are on your own you need to have a clear understanding from the beginning on how you will handle customer care. In either case, this means that you need to be proactive in knowing exactly who can help if one of your customers has an issue that needs to be taken care of. We cannot emphasize enough how important it is to be available to your customers either by e-mail or phone so they know someone is there who cares. Head off any issues before they become big problems by following up with the hostess after the party just to make sure all is well. Let her know once again that if anyone needs anything at all you are available.

We believe that if someone has a complaint, it is a valid one and we should address it. In the past we have sometimes jumped through hoops to get a product to a person who ended up wanting to return it because it was not what she thought it was going to be, and we had to take it back. But guess what? That person is still our customer. We pride ourselves on being there when our customers need us, and providing the service that they need when they need it. If our reps have a complaint we handle it through our corporate office. Not only does this show the rep's customer that we are a professional company interested in making them happy, it shows our reps that they are not in business by themselves and they are involved with a company that cares about them as well. We have had reps join us from other sex-toy party companies just because of our return policy, as they had experienced problems in the past.

Our suggestion is to think as follows: The customer is always right. Most people will not tell you that something doesn't work or is broken unless it really *is* broken. Replace the item; it will bring good will. If someone doesn't like something, offer to exchange it, even if it comes out of your own pocket. If someone calls to complain about not receiving their order or to say their order was wrong, listen to the customer and don't argue. Apologize and make it right. If you screwed up, admit it and fix it. Follow this philosophy and you will have satisfied customers and a successful business.

FIVE

Girlfriends Are a Girl's Best Friend: Network Marketing & Finding More Customers

O nce you have your business up and running, it's time to get out there and party! With customers, that is. To find your customers, sell your products and earn that big income you've been dreaming about, you need to book parties. Lots of them. So, where do you start?

Reach Out and Touch Someone!

The easiest place to start booking is with your family and friends. Tell everybody that you know, everyone you meet, people who are acquaintances through other friends, and the people *they* know that you are a sex-toy party representative. Tell them you would *love* to come into their homes and show their friends your fabulous product line. Explain how much

fun having a sex-toy party is, and let them know the hostess
benefits. (Hopefully you have chosen a company that gives nice
perks to the hostess for all her work). Be warm, positive and
enthusiastic because if you are excited, they will get excited
too. Make yourself approachable and accessible. Make sure
they have your phone number or business card with all your
contact information. Simply talking about the benefits of
having a party is an effective way of building your business.

- **Phone your friends.** Tell them you're calling with good
  news: you've got a new business with great potential
  for you *and* them!

- **Send out announcement postcards.** Print postcards
  with your company's logo on one side and a general
  message with your contact info on the back. There
  are a number of companies online that produce these
  inexpensively and professionally.

- **Don't forget the power of e-mail.** Put your e-mail list
  together and blast away. Be enthusiastic, as people
  catch on to your commitment to your business.
  Encourage them to share the news with other friends
  so they know what the "buzz" is all about. Just beware the words you use, since most people's spam fil-
  ters will catch sex-related terminology.

- **Throw an introductory party.** Invite all your friends
  and family over and introduce them to the sex-toy
  party concept with your own demonstration. Let them
  know that you are available for their gatherings and
  encourage them to spread the word.

- **Keep your ears open.** Bachelorette, birthday, girls'
  night out and similar celebrations are all perfect oc-

casions for a sex-toy party. When you hear of such events coming up, let people know that you can provide this fun and sexy service.

Set Your Goals and Perfect Your Pitch

In any business, particularly one that depends on self-motivation, it is important to set clear goals. These goals are your roadmap: they spell out where you are going and what your expectations are. When starting out, you should set goals for:

- The number of phone calls you will make each day, whether they are initial contact calls or follow-up calls.
- The number of parties you will book per week.
- The number of parties you expect to book from each party.

When you start a sex-toy party business, you need to understand that it takes a lot of work and dedication to build your business. Success does not happen overnight. We have met so many women who spend good money on their kits and think it will be easy to start repping, only to discover it is not. Before signing up with any company, or starting your very own business, make sure you understand *why* you are getting into business for yourself. There is a saying that independent business owners have: "If it was easy, everyone would be doing it!"

You need to make sure that your goals fit your personality. Are you outgoing? Do you like to network? Then you will probably be out there talking up your business. If you are a quiet, shy person you will probably start out slower and build your business with friends and family. Be aware of your comfort and skill level, and be honest with your expectations from there. Don't put so much pressure on yourself that it becomes self-defeating; you will never win that game. Be realistic about your capabilities and go with that. Remember, this is *your* business, whichever way you decide to go, so ultimately you decide your destiny. If you think about it, that's a very powerful concept! Whatever your goals are, we have information that will help you either make the decision to start your own company or join an established sex-toy party company.

The next step is to set goals for how many parties you will book from the guests of a previous party. The primary way a rep increases her hostess-and-customer base is through successful parties. We recommend beginning with a goal to book two parties from each party that you serve. As your network grows and you improve your services, you might increase your goal to five bookings from every party, but it is important to set achievable goals at first and be successful. Do not have such high expectations that you become discouraged and want to give up.

Prepare your pitch for booking parties so you can present it to the guests after you have completed your presentation. If you don't talk about your availability at every party, guests may not realize that your parties are available to them as well. Tell yourself as you close each party that you need to book at least one party from this party. Then schmooze enthusiastically with any interested guests and follow up with them after the party. Do this consistently, and you will build a solid business over time.

There are several appropriate times during the course of an evening to give the guests a party pitch. The first is when you are finishing the demonstration. Let them know that if they liked this presentation, you are available to all of them for their parties in the future. The second opportunity is when you are taking each individual's order and have time to connect with interested guests one-on-one.

A pitch at the end of the party may sound something like this: "Thank you for coming to Suzie's tonight and giving me the chance to introduce you to these fabulous sexy things. I hope that you all had a lot of fun! To let you know how our home parties work, as a thank you for inviting us into her home for this party, Suzie will earn $X in free products from My Party Company. She will also receive an additional $X for each party that is booked with me from this party. So think about this…you can have a fun party, receive free sexy products, and help your friend earn more money if you book a party with me. So, who is having the next party?!"

We like to mention hostess benefits to the partygoers because it gives them multiple incentives to throw a party of their own. In addition to the appealing hostess gifts and financial incentive, they learn that by throwing their own party they will also benefit their friend.

Focus on the Follow-Up

When booking parties, follow-up is the key to success. You need to be in consistent and persistent with people interested in booking a party. Follow-up is important for getting a party commitment and nailing down a specific date. Good follow-up also sends the message to your customer that you are a professional who is available to them. This sets the stage for a positive sex-toy party experience.

Keep in mind that there is a fine line between being persistent and going overboard with your follow-up. Our rule of thumb is to call three times. When you first get a call from an interested hostess, make sure to call back as soon as you get her message. If you haven't heard back within 24 hours, try her again. If you still haven't heard anything after another two days, make your third call. If you haven't heard back after three calls, let it go and move on. She may be signaling that she has changed her mind. More than three calls is a waste of your time and might become annoying to your potential customer. Some people say they are interested in having a party, but later realize they are not willing to put the time into it and don't know how to back out. So cut your hostess some slack.

A big obstacle that many of us in the sex-toy party business face is how to not get personally involved. Booking parties is not a popularity contest. People have unexpected things come up in their lives; if they don't follow through or have to cancel it's nothing personal. As a professional, you just have to remain objective but open. Rejection is part of this business. Keep yourself available to everyone, even those who have been hesitant or had to cancel. You never know when someone will reappear and book a party with you.

Good follow-up is a form of marketing yourself—and if you do this successfully, you'll have a solid business. The message that you want to get across to your customers is that you are available to meet their needs. *You are your business.* Home parties do not happen without you. Once you have figured this out, and you have parties booking off of parties successfully, and you are starting to make a name for yourself, pat yourself on the back! Then, begin to think about whether you want to grow your business. If so, you can turn your attentions to expanding your marketing.

Taking It to the Next Level: Advertising

Another way to market yourself is by placing localized and Internet advertising. Advertising can be very effective, but it can also be very costly. Advertising is also known for being hit-and-miss. You may receive immediate results after you run an ad, or you may not receive results for six months. In fact, you may not get any results at all. The best thing that you can do when you're considering advertising is to approach it cautiously and do your research. Outline exactly who you want to target with the ads, then ask potential publications for their readership's demographics. If they don't match, don't place the ad. With advertising, as with any marketing expense, you want to make sure that your costs are in line with the benefits. This will only happen if the readership of your ads are women who are interested in sex-toy party activities.

On the subject of research again (can you tell we're big on this?), we know that you would like to think that all women would like to have a sex-toy party, but this is just not the case. It is a really special, open woman who is willing to have dildos and other sensual items displayed all over her tables and discussed in her home, so you are going to want to find a way to reach that person effectively. Our suggestion would be to ask women who have had a sex-toy party or who have attended one of your parties what local newspapers or magazine they read. If you can figure this out for your local market, then you will probably do well with your advertising.

Text continued on page 70.

MEASURING YOUR RESULTS

Make sure that you have created a way to measure your results so that you know where your new business is coming from. Put together a little questionnaire so that you know how each hostess and customer has found you. This will help you determine which marketing initiatives are working for you.

By the phone, you can keep a list of questions to ask new customers—"How did you hear about us: Reading an ad? Word of mouth?" Demographic information (a person's age, income, interests, etc.) is very useful, but many people feel those questions are too personal, and don't want to answer. You'll have to get a sense of how open the person is as you talk on the phone. Once you build up a nice rapport it's much easier to get information out of a person.

See facing page for an example of a questionnaire we sent to customers in the mail. Mailed questionnaires usually get a smaller response, unless you're offering an attractive incentive (for example, *Return the questionnaire to receive a free bottle of massage oil!*). You can also call customers directly to ask for information—the personal connection is more likely to yield a response. To keep track of the information, make up a simple chart in Excel and go through the responses weekly to see how you are getting business.

Another great idea is to do a cost/benefit analysis of your advertising. First figure out how much it costs to place the ad (let's say $300). Then figure out how many phone calls you received from it (let's say 30 calls). You can then determine how much each call cost you (30 calls for $300 = $10 per call). If you book a party or two from those calls, then look at your sales total for those parties. If you made more than $300 from the parties, then your ad was worth the original $300 investment. This type of analysis will help you see whether your marketing efforts are successful and decide whether you should continue them.

Sample Questionnaire

I. How did you find our ad?

❑ Yahoo   ❑ Google   ❑ Alta Vista

❑ Lycos   ❑ US Magazine ad   ❑ Soap Opera Digest

❑ Redbook Magazine   ❑ Word of mouth

❑ Other _____

2. What other publications do you read on a regular basis? (regular basis means at least once a month)

Publications_____

3. Are you: ❑ Male   ❑ Female

4. Are you: ❑ Married   ❑ Single, never married

              ❑ Divorced   ❑ Widowed

5. Which of the following age categories are you in?

❑ Under 25   ❑ 25–34

❑ 35–44   ❑ 45–54

❑ 55–64   ❑ 65 or older

6. What is your yearly household income before taxes?

❑ Less than $25,000

❑ $25,000–$49,000

❑ $50,000–$74,000

❑ $75,000–$99,000

❑ $100,000 or more

7. Any Additional Comments:

_____

_____

_____

_____

_____

Find Your Roots: Grassroots Marketing

Investing in advertising is not the only way to get your name out there. There are as many methods of grassroots marketing as there are marketers. You will need to discover which ones work for you. Be creative and open-minded with your marketing. There are a number of books out there on marketing on a shoestring budget and "guerrilla marketing" (a way to market creatively for less money). In the meantime, here are a few ideas to get you started.

- **Make a donation.** Put together a gift basket full of your less risqué items and donate it to a local fundraiser to be auctioned off. This can turn the recipient into a customer and it is a relatively inexpensive way to get advertising and exposure.

- **Join a networking group.** There are plenty of networking groups that cater specifically to women business owners. You can find them online or in your local yellow pages. A great resource to find networking groups for women online is www.wwwomen.com. Check with your local Chamber of Commerce for networking events and other opportunities to build your business. Such events are all good places to hand out business cards. We have been to women's networking groups where you can buy a time slot and spend 15 minutes speaking about your business. We usually spend part of the time explaining the benefits of having a party as well as the parties themselves, in hopes of recruiting hostesses, customers and other reps.

- **Attend local conventions**. There are many local conventions that deal specifically with women's issues. You can rent a booth and have women sign up if they are interested in hosting a party or starting a business of their own (you will follow up later). Many times you can provide items for auction at these events, or sponsor specific speakers. We have even seen opportunities for break out sessions where you can speak at these events about issues that face women.

- **Post small ads on home business websites**. There are a multitude of websites that deal with home business opportunities for women. You might even be able to find local sites in your area where you can post advertisements. Two sites to check out that have designated areas to post business opportunities for women are www.bizoffice.com and www.powehouse biz.com.

- **Get on the home-party circuit**. By attending home parties for other products such as Pampered Chef, Mary Kay and the like, you will meet women who already understand the party concept and are buying from home parties. These are perfect candidates for your pitches.

- **Hook up with referral sources**. Make connections with referral sources within your community. For you this might be a lingerie boutique, a neighborhood florist or a bridal shop. Ask if they will refer you to their customers or display your business cards on their counter.

- **Consider co-op marketing.** Co-op marketing is simply sharing the cost of marketing your business with another business whereby you both benefit from the "partnership." For instance, if you hook up with a good referral source like a local lingerie boutique and they want to do a local advertisement, you can share in those costs, and in return have your business mentioned in the ad along with them. Or if you have a good connection with another local business that caters to your target market, such as a health spa or beauty salon, talk with them about co-oping into one of their promotions.

Your marketing needs to be based on what you want the outcome to be. For example, if your goal for marketing is to expand party bookings, that will require different actions than if you are looking to build a "downline" and recruit more representatives to work beneath you. Before you embark on marketing initiatives, have it very clear on paper what your goals are and what you expect to accomplish, and then map out the best path to get there.

Develop a Mailing List

When taking orders from customers, it is always important to get as much personal information (address, telephone number, e-mail address) as possible. Gathering this information not only gives you a way to contact them about their order, but it will help you build a repeat customer base and a growing pool of referrals for future parties. It also creates a mailing list for you, which is a terrific marketing tool.

When building your mailing list, it is important that you ask for your customers' permission to contact them by mail or e-mail. Sending postcards or flyers to people who have not requested to be on your mailing list can be annoying at best and embarrassing or unwelcome at worst. Remember that while sensational sex is your business and you are proud to spread the word about it, for many people sex it is still a private affair. Many of your customers might want to keep their bedroom interests away from children or other family members.

Also understand that e-mails sent without explicit permission are considered spam. If you are caught sending spam, you can be reported to your e-mail provider and they can close down your e-mail account. More importantly, as a customer-oriented businesswoman you don't want to risk alienating anyone, because the chances of you receiving another order from that person will be slim to none.

Here are suggestions for building a voluntary, or "opt-in," mailing list:

- At the close of each party, add a short comment about your newsletter and the benefits of receiving it. Explain the type of information you will be sending: special discounts, holiday promotions, health information— whatever you have in mind. Later when you take individual orders, ask each customer if she would like to be added to your mailing list.

- Give a small gift to all who sign up for your newsletter. Make it something affordable for you. Ideally, it should be something you don't carry in your kit, so

EXAMPLE OF A LADY BLISS "HOST A PARTY" LETTER

Host a Lady Bliss Home Party
and Have a Fantastic Time!

What's a Lady Bliss home party? It's a new twist on things...
Having a girls' night out? What's cooler than a Tupperware party, more seductive than cosmetics, and more fun than a poker game? A Lady Bliss home party—that's what!

The Lady Bliss commitment...
The definition of bliss..."Being in a complete state of happiness, a state of euphoria." At Lady Bliss we are committed to celebrating and enhancing this state of being by providing women from all walks of life a way to elevate and enhance their romantic lives and individual sexuality in a safe and enriching environment. Lady Bliss is truly dedicated to providing a shopping experience that is free from pornographic imagery and offering quality products that are packaged and presented to you in the same spirit. We want women to feel not only confident but proud to be shopping from our catalog, website and home parties.

Why should you have a Lady Bliss home party?
Because they're fun, fabulously discreet and profitable—that's why! When you have a Lady Bliss home party you learn new and exciting

people feel they are getting something that no one else can buy from you.

- Give an additional discount for signing up at the party. Consider giving 5 to 10 percent off their total order at the party, or off a future order. (Make sure beforehand that you can afford to give this discount, since it will come out of your bottom line.)

ways to use top-quality romantic products to help enhance your love life. The Lady Bliss product line is shown and sold to you and your friends by an experienced Lady Bliss home party representative in the privacy of your home, while you earn great gifts and incentives just for having fun!

How does a Lady Bliss home party work for you?
By hosting a Lady Bliss home party you are able to earn fabulous discounts on all of your own Lady Bliss purchases. Depending on the total sales of your party you may also be eligible to earn additional gifts.

For having a Lady Bliss home party you will receive...
• 10% of the total party sales toward your personal purchases. In other words, if the party total is $300 (not including sales tax and shipping fees) you will receive a credit for $30.
• For every guest who books a home party and holds her party within 60 days of yours, you will receive $25 per sign-up in additional shopping credits toward more Lady Bliss merchandise and she will receive a free gift!
• You receive free gifts too!

And the best part is the party comes directly to you!
Give us a call today so you can host your very own Lady Bliss home party tomorrow! 866-352-5477

• Add a space on your order sheets with a check box saying "Yes! I want to receive your monthly newsletter." This way you have a document stating that they have agreed to receive it.
• Have a sign-up sheet for partygoers who do not order but who want to be alerted to your special promotions.

EXAMPLE OF A LADY BLISS NEWSLETTER

Are you ready for Valentine's Day? If you can't answer that question have no fear—Lady Bliss is here! We have some great last minute romance ideas just for you, along with some very special gifts wrapped and ready for romance! With our beautiful collection of **Gift Baskets, Romance Products, Sexy Adult Toys, Erotic Viewing** and our newest addition, **Lingerie**, we have your romantic gift-giving covered! Free shipping on orders $25 or more too! Make sure to order by **February 11th** to ensure your products arrive on time for V-Day! **Overnight and 2-day shipping available for in-stock items for an additional shipping fee!**

Lingerie Is a Great Gift for Him and for Her!

What is it about **Lingerie** that makes a woman look so beautiful and a man so turned on? Is it the way the woman's body curves so beautifully within the sheer fabric showing her nakedness, yet covering it up? Or is it the man's anticipation of taking it off, a little bit at a time, while nibbling and fondling her? Whatever the reason, Lady Bliss has what you both are looking for. Feminine, sheer, sexy and alluring describes our wonderful collection of **Lingerie**. Take a peek…you'll like what you see!

Strip Tease Anyone?

Why not surprise your lover with a sexy striptease? In a private room just for the two of you, wear your sexy lingerie (like our **Black Baby Doll** and matching thong) and have seductive music playing in the back-

DIRECT MAIL

Direct mail refers to anything that you send through regular mail. Postcards, catalogs and one-page flyers or newsletters are all mailers that you might find useful. You can use these to promote annual sales, special offers, reminders for Valentine's Day shopping and so forth. (See above and page 74 for exam-

ground. Sit your lover down on a chair and straddle his lap with your legs while rubbing against his body with yours. Let your body move to the music while stripping off his clothes, one piece at a time, letting him do the same. You will have an erotic night you both won't soon forget! For great stripping tips check out **How to Strip** in our video section.

An Aphrodisiac Dinner for Two Please!

Why not make a sexy dinner with deliciously seductive foods? As you prepare the meal together, feed each other as you chop, dice and sauté. Take time to taste and feel the allure of a tomato or the creaminess and sweetness of milk chocolate. Lie down and sample the ingredients on each other. Make this meal like no other you have ever done in the past! For great aphrodisiac cooking ideas buy *Intercourses, an Aphrodisiac Cookbook.*

Free Gift for Orders $50 and Over!

Just in time for Valentine's Day! Receive your free gift, 52 WEEKS OF ROMANCE, for orders of $50 or more. Lady Bliss wants to make sure you have the most romantic Valentine's Day ever by offering new and sensual ways to seduce the one you love. Don't miss out—offer ends February 14th! **(Please mention "Valentine's offer" in the order comments.)**

**Lady Bliss wishes you a Valentine's Day
full of *caring*, *sharing* and being *daring*!**

ples.) When considering whether or not to do a direct mailing, you should take into account the cost of the printing, the postage and your time to print out labels or handwrite addresses. Then weigh these against your goals for the mailing—how many direct sales you expect and how many parties you would like to book—to make sure that it's a good investment.

E-MAIL AND SNAIL MAIL MARKETING

E-mail is an effective yet inexpensive way to build your business. With your e-mail list you may want to consider doing a monthly newsletter. There are services available that will send out newsletters on a monthly basis for a fee. However, you can create something on your own inexpensively and send it out yourself. If you don't have enough information for a monthly newsletter, send one out bi-monthly. Some of the information you may want to include in your newsletter are monthly specials that you are offering, new hostess gifts for throwing a party, promotional events or anything health related that you think your customers should know about. The focus of your e-mail can vary each time. One issue may feature a promotion while the next month you share beneficial information. (See page 76 for an example.)

Having your customers' home mailing addresses allows you to send them invitations to a special event you are having, recognize a holiday or a birthday (if you have a close enough relationship with them) or mail out your newsletter instead of e-mailing it (however, this is more expensive to do). You may also want to send out company catalogs close to the holidays, or send coupons for dollars off a particular product or for purchases over a certain amount. If you have a website, consider sending coupons for spending a certain amount on your website.

Even if they get you just one repeat sale or one party, these marketing efforts will be worth it, but we caution you to be patient. Sometimes it takes a few attempts to get any response. The most important thing about e-mail marketing is that you are keeping yourself visible to your customer base, so when they think of romantic products, they will purchase them from you.

Marketing is one of the most important things you can do to build a successful sex-toy home party business. Whether you want to have a huge sex-toy party business or a smaller part-time business, you must get out there and spread the word or you will never have success. Don't expect huge things to happen right away, though! We cannot emphasize this enough. We have seen it happen time and time again: women who have signed up to be Lady Bliss sex-toy party reps talk to a few people, but things don't work out the way they planned, and they walk away because it was harder than they had anticipated. This business is like any other business—it takes work. The misconception seems to be that because most sex-toy party businesses are relatively simple to get into and do not require an investment of thousands of dollars, the job must be easy. Think again: it's an opportunity, and what you put into it is what you will get out of it.

PART THREE

Down & Dirty: Choosing the Business Structure That's Right for You

If you are seriously thinking about starting your own sex-toy party business, it's time to investigate the structure your business should take. There are lots of different ways to set up a business, including sole proprietorships, partnerships, limited liability companies and corporations. How do you know which is right for you?

The structure that your business should take depends primarily on how big you want it to be. What are your goals? Do you want to rep part-time for another company? Start a small solo business from scratch? Build a large business with your own reps? Or become a millionaire sex-toy tycoon? The best business structure for you will also depend on how you plan to finance your business. Will you go it alone or will you bring in a partner? Will you seek investment money from outside your company?

Before diving in to this new venture, it is vital to think everything through so that when you do take the plunge you are poised for success. In the next three chapters, we offer general insights and nitty-gritty details about the business decision-making process so that you can determine which form of business is just right for you.

SIX

Rep Rap:
Repping for a
Home-Party Company

Working as a representative for an established sex-toy party company is a great way to get your feet wet and explore the business, whether your goal is to grow as a rep or eventually branch out and start your very own sex-toy party company. One of the benefits of repping is that you have flexibility to determine just how much time you want to put into the business—part time or full time. Being a rep is the perfect option for women who want to make a little money on the side, who just want to work weekends or who need flexible hours to raise a family. It is also ideal for women who want to work full time but don't want to start their own company.

As a rep for an existing company, you reap the benefits of not having to build a company from scratch. For example, you do not have to raise capital, set up an office, create marketing materials, manage public relations or invest large amounts of money into the business during the (often lengthy) time it takes to become profitable. Repping eliminates all the headaches of launching a start-up. As a rep, you buy into a "turn-key operation"—and it is really worth it!

Marketing Benefits

An established sex-toy party company has already identified their market, conducted research on what works for that market and developed a company brand identity. As their rep, you don't need to do that work…you just need to *work it*. Repping lets you step right in and focus on what you do best: sell!

MARKETING MATERIALS

Each sex-toy party company has spent time and energy to create attractive, quality marketing materials such as business cards, catalogs, invitations and so forth that will appeal to their audience. As a rep working for them, you have access to these materials so you don't need to develop your own. The sex-toy party companies we profile on pages 94–97 all include basic marketing materials in their initial kit, and you can purchase additional materials directly from them. (Note the flip side to this: most sex-toy party companies require that their company image and marketing messages be consistent and legal, which means they must control or approve everything that goes out with their name on it. As a result, most do not allow reps to distribute their own marketing materials without corporate approval.)

PUBLICITY

Publicity can have a huge impact on the business, building credibility and name recognition. This, in turn, gives company reps better opportunity to book parties. Publicity can be an ongoing, costly and time-consuming expense. As a rep, you enjoy the benefits of your company's publicity efforts without having to solicit the media yourself. Publicity is usually handled directly by the corporate office. In fact, some companies prohibit their reps from speaking to the press without corporate approval. They do this to ensure that all branding and messages from the company are clear, consistent and legal. Since the press can also turn a business upside down, the message that is sent out through publicity is very important.

ADVERTISING

Many but not all of the top sex-toy party companies advertise. Advertising can build name recognition for a company, but it can also be a huge expense and may not always be the best way to reach an audience. In many cases, advertising is the expense that kills an independent company. Most party companies will work with reps who are interested in advertising, and most will provide you with approved templates for ads. For example, Lady Bliss pre-approves advertisements and then shares in the costs of pre-approved ads if we are looking to gain market segment in that area. For reps, advertising is usually not advisable unless you know exactly what you hope to gain from the advertising—and can afford to spend the money knowing that it may not result in any sales.

WEBSITES

The Internet is an increasingly important tool for the sex-toy party businesses. All of the larger, more established companies have at minimum a site for their corporate entity. Many have sites that sell directly to customers and provide information for hostesses and representatives. Having a web presence builds credibility for the company by advertising their services, their products and the principles behind their company philosophy. These websites can be a huge help for bringing parties and orders to the top reps in the company. Most company websites offer a sign-up form for hostesses to request a party. They also field requests from people interested in becoming a representative. And some of the sites sell party kits.

A potential rep should look for a professional, user-friendly site where this information is easy to find. This way you can proudly send potential hostesses to the site when you are recruiting them. Ideally, your company should not offer direct ordering from their site unless there is a way for customers to input

TALES FROM LADY BLISS LIFE

One of our Lady Bliss reps always takes her laptop to her home parties. This way if someone is looking for something specific or if guests just want to look at the entire Lady Bliss catalog online they can. This always increases her orders—a rep can never carry enough in her kit to keep everyone happy.

your name so that you get credit for the sale. Otherwise, you are simply competing with them for sales.

At Lady Bliss, our reps can set up their own websites to help them market and make sales. These websites can be set up either within Lady Bliss (such as www.ladybliss.com/jane-smith) or at a rep's own URL (such a www.janesmithparties. com). The reps' sites work in such a way that their customers can shop our entire catalog, offering much more than each rep's party kit, and the rep will receive a commission on all the sales. One of our reps who actively promotes her website gets an average of one to two extra orders each month just from the website.

Business Structure Benefits

When you sign up as a rep for a sex-toy party company, it is very much like owning your own franchise. You are buying into a turn-key operation under the umbrella of a larger company, but in fact you run your own office as your see fit.

SOLE PROPRIETORSHIPS

Repping for an established company allows you to benefit from the simplest business structure available: a sole proprietorship. This structure has the simplest tax reporting and requires the least amount of paperwork and effort. All income that you receive from your business can be reported under your social security number. You don't need to worry about registering for a Federal Tax ID number and may not even need a business license. (See A Note on Paperwork, page 89.) Sole proprietorship is an appropriate structure for most small enterprises. We recommend it for anyone considering this as a part-time endeavor.

If you are you are planning on repping on a full-time basis, however, we suggest that you consider obtaining a DBA ("Doing Business As") and a Federal Tax ID number for your new company. Doing so establishes your business as a separate entity with its own name and accounts.

PARTNERSHIPS AND CORPORATIONS

Many sex-toy party companies give you the option to sign up as a "partnership" or a "corporation." If you are looking to enter into a representative agreement with a friend and share the workload, then you should enter into a partnership agreement and get a Federal Tax ID number for the partnership. Your partnership agreement needs to cover how you plan on handling expenses, splitting the revenue and sharing the workload, among other things. Never enter into a business with another individual without putting some type of written agreement in place. If you are already running another direct sales company, you may wish to consider setting yourself up as a corporation so that you can report all of your businesses together. Remember, there can be significant tax ramifications when owning your own company. If you are unsure or have questions about any of this, ask a certified public accountant (CPA). The more complicated your business structure, the more significant your tax, legal and accounting costs will be.

BOOKKEEPING AND TAXES

Being a rep for most sex-toy party companies is a lot like having your own company in terms of your income, book-

A NOTE ON PAPERWORK

You may or may not need a business license depending upon the state, county and city in which you live. You can usually find this information at your local city hall. It is a good idea to create a DBA ("Doing Business As") for your business to establish some separation between yourself and your company.

When you conduct your business as a sole proprietorship, all the accounting will use your name and your social security number. When you have a DBA, you have a Federal Tax ID number and can run the business under any name. As a DBA, you have flexibility in naming your sexy new enterprise.

At the very least, you need to open a separate bank account for your business. Commingling business and personal funds can be a fast ticket to failure and will make an IRS audit extremely painful. Even as a part-time rep, once your annual gross sales are greater than $600 you will receive a 1099-MISC report of income. This goes to the IRS and your state government. It is important that you do these basic things to set yourself up for being in business, because you are in business.

The good news is that as a business you can deduct all of your related expenses when you do your income taxes—but you have to be ready to prove your income and expenses. Thus record keeping is very important since it reduces the overall taxes you have to pay. Since we don't cover tax law or accounting in this book, we suggest you check out books on small business accounting. They will cover everything you need to know. Some of our favorites are:

- *The Girl's Guide to Starting Your Own Business* by Caitlin Friedman and Kimberly Yorio
- *Start Your Own Business: The Only Start-Up Book You Will Ever Need* by Rieva Lesonsky
- *The Business Start-Up Kit* by Steven D. Strauss.

keeping and tax structures. As a rep, you are considered an "independent contractor." This means that the income you receive from your host company will be reported to the IRS at the end of the year on the form 1099-MISC Income (similar to a W-2 but for companies and individuals who are not employees). You need to understand that income taxes and social security taxes will not be withheld by the host company, so you will have to pay them yourself, directly to the IRS, on an annual or quarterly basis based on your net income ("net income" is the money you actually make after your business expenses have been deducted from your income). What all this means is that you have the same bookkeeping requirements that you would have when running any type of business. If you are a sole proprietor, come tax time you will need to file a Schedule C form, which accounts for your business income and your business expenses.

GROWTH OPPORTUNITIES/MULTILEVEL OPPORTUNITIES

Many sex-toy party companies have multilevel plans for high-powered reps who want to build a line of reps underneath them. Multilevel plans offer the opportunity to have your own distribution team working for you (you end up running a sales team but not a company). Most multilevel companies will give you a percentage of the sales made by the reps that you recruit. Thus, if you sign up three reps, you may make as much as 5 percent of their sales every month. As independent reps, however, they are not under your control; your role is to be a team leader and help them to grow into productive salespeople. This is why you receive a percentage of their income. If your company pays down multiple levels, you will also earn a percentage of the sales from any reps your reps recruit (usually 1 to 2 percent). In this industry, very few companies pay more than two levels deep because the profitability margins are slim.

Many women in multilevel party companies, such as Mary Kay, Pampered Chef and Party Lite, earn six-figure incomes by building a strong distribution team below them. The main risk to building a distribution team under the framework of a company that is not your own, is that you have no real control over what happens if the main company is sold or goes out of business. Should one of these things happen, your best recourse is to try and move your entire team to a different multilevel company.

OVERHEAD

What overhead? As a rep, the only overhead you have is the roof over yours! Working as a rep means that you don't have monthly overhead expenses of an established company—just your own home business. So you don't have to worry about office space, warehouse space, packing materials, shipping costs, payroll, payroll taxes and so forth (expenses that typically run at 4 percent to 20 percent of a company's sales).

LEGAL ISSUES

Depending on where you live, selling these sexy, adult products could be in violation of local decency laws. Decency laws vary by locality, and they vary greatly. A good party company should make you aware of any laws that are applicable in your area. We know that you are good, decent folk dedicated to bringing people happiness and healthy relationships, and some of these states do too. Even states with decency laws will likely look the other way; many will only bother you if you've received a complaint. In any case, be aware of your local regulations.

As a rep, you don't need to worry much about other legal issues. Your party company will provide you with general liability protection from the products. Additionally, as a rep you will also sign a distribution agreement with the party company, so make sure that you read it carefully as this is a binding legal document. And that's about it!

If you are carrying inventory, check with your homeowners and auto insurance to see if the products are covered in your home or in your car. Most homeowner policies will not cover products that you carry for a business, so if you have inventory you may need to purchase an additional rider to cover the value of your inventory. If you don't carry inventory (i.e. if your company takes care of distribution for you), then you don't need to worry about this.

Finding the Company That Is Right for You

If you decide to go the rep route, take the time to do your homework and check out a variety of different companies before making a decision. The key to your success is to work with the company that is the best match for you.

There are some simple things you can do to identify the company that is right for you:

- Host a party to check them out.
- Get expert opinions. Ask for the names and phone numbers of several active representatives and talk to them about their experiences with the company.
- Visit their corporate websites and see how long it takes for someone to respond to your questions—you may be surprised!
- Purchase something and test out their customer service. Do you like the way they handle web, phone and party orders? Did they thoughtfully answer customer service questions? Do you like their return policy?
- Review the company philosophy and see if it is in line with your basic philosophies about sex and relationships.
- Review their product line. Are you going to be comfortable selling their items? Are you passionate about their products?
- Evaluate how they stack up to your needs: time, cash flow, return on investment.

We have created the "Compensation Comparison of the Major Party Companies" on pages 94–97 to assist you in this search.

Text continued on page 98.

COMPENSATION COMPARISON
OF THE MAJOR PARTY COMPANIES

This chart highlights the major compensation areas of each of the party companies mentioned in this book. It is intended as an overview, is not all-inclusive, and should not be used as your sole decision-making tool. We recommend that prior to signing up with any company as a party rep or hostess, you thoroughly research the time, energy and financial commitment you will be making.

	SLUMBER PARTIES	PASSION PARTIES	FANTASY LADY	LADY BLISS
START-UP COSTS	3 kits available: $250, $500 or $1000. Shipping is extra. Business cards and order forms included in each kit.	3 kits available: $100, $250 or $450. Shipping is extra. Business aids included in each kit. Multimedia Business Center free with $250 and $450 kits.	4 kits available: $250, $500, $1000 or $1250. Shipping is extra. Catalogs and order forms included in all kits. Additional business aids included in the more expensive kits.	1 main kit available: $395. Shipping is extra. Order forms, brochures, invitations and business cards included. 5 add-on kits available (cost from $25 to $225): Lingerie, books, videos, romance, additional sex toys, truth or dare.
BUYING DISCOUNTS	Reps buy merchandise at 40% off retail price.	Reps buy merchandise at 10% off retail price on $100 kit; 25% on $250 kit; 40% on $450 kit. To increase your buying discount from 10% to 40% you must place one order of $300 retail and an additional order of $1000 retail.	Reps buy merchandise at 30% off retail price on $250 kit; 35% on $500 kit; 40% on $1000 kit; and 50% on $1250 kit.	Reps do not buy merchandise: a 20% commission is paid on all customer orders you solicit, whether they come from a home party, your Lady Bliss website or a catalog sale.

	SLUMBER PARTIES	PASSION PARTIES	FANTASY LADY	LADY BLISS
TRAINING BONUS FOR RECRUITING NEW REPS	10% of the price of each kit sold.	Sponsor a new consultant who becomes a qualified consultant within 60 days and receive a one-time $30 bonus.	Earn bonus reward points for each recruit you sign up. For every 5 recruits, receive a merit bonus of 20,000 points.	$100 for each new recruit you train. $100 additional bonus once that rep has held a party with sales of $300.
HANDLING ORDERS: WHO DOES WHAT?	Rep buys products at discount from the company, handles inventory and is responsible for delivering products to customers.	Rep buys products at discount from the company, handles inventory and is responsible for getting products to customers.	Rep buys products at discount from the company, handles inventory and is responsible for getting products to customers.	Company handles all order processing and ships directly to customers. Rep is responsible for sending orders to the company.
DOWNLINE SALES PERCENTAGES AND OVERRIDES	You earn an override (a percentage of sales) for each rep you personally recruit, for each rep recruited by one of your reps, and each rep those reps recruit. (i.e., 3 levels down) The percentage you earn ranges from 2%–4% depending on monthly sales volume and number of distributors under you.	You earn an override (a percentage of sales) for each rep you personally recruit, for each rep recruited by one of your reps, and each rep those reps recruit. (i.e., 3 levels down) The percentage you earn ranges from 5%–15% depending upon monthly sales volume and number of distributors under you.	You earn an override (a percentage of sales) of 3% for each rep you recruit, an override of 2% for each rep recruited by one of your reps, an override of 1% for each rep those reps recruit, and an override of 0.5% for each rep those reps recruit. (i.e., the override goes down 4 levels)	You earn an override (a percentage of sales) of 5% on all personal recruits, one level deep only. No multilevels. Regional Sales Manager can earn an additional 5% override.

	SLUMBER PARTIES	PASSION PARTIES	FANTASY LADY	LADY BLISS
WHAT YOU NEED TO STAY QUALIFIED	To qualify you must place your first retail order of $250 within 30 days of the original kit ship date. To stay active, you must purchase at least $200 in retail two consecutive months in a row.	To qualify you must place a $250 retail sales volume within your first 60 days. To stay active, you must purchase $600 in retail during any rolling 6-month period.	If you make no retail purchases in a 6-month period, then you must purchase a minimum of $100 in retail to reactivate.	No qualifications at this time.
FREE PRODUCTS OR CASH BONUSES	All qualified distributors are eligible to receive free products. Free products are dependent upon your retail level, which must be over $1000. Free products also depend on the number of recruits you bring in.	Cash bonuses are based on a calendar month with retail sales greater than $2000.	"Rep-rewards" points can be accumulated for free products.	Bonus incentives available based on sales volume.
WEBSITES FOR REPS	No	Yes: $25 per month fee.	No	Personalized home page that links to the Lady Bliss main site: no extra fee.

	SLUMBER PARTIES	PASSION PARTIES	FANTASY LADY	LADY BLISS
ADDITIONAL COMPENSATION AVAILABLE	Check with the company for more information.	Car allowance of $400 per month available to reps with: personal retail sales of $1500, total group sales of $36,000 (of which $5000 are first level), and 15 active personally-sponsored qualified consultants. You must achieve these requirements each month for 4 consecutive months.	Rep-Rewards program in which you can earn points in every aspect of your business. There are no levels to this program. Points never expire.	Fast-Start program and sales volume bonuses. Incentive programs.

EVALUATING YOUR NEEDS

We suggest you think carefully and honestly about your needs, your talents, your interests and your finances as you search for a sex-toy party company. Each company works with their reps differently, in terms of the initial financial investment you will need to make, how they compensate you, how they support you and how you can grow within the company.

Ask yourself the following questions and spend some time thinking about the answers. You might even want to write down the answers in a notebook or journal, so you have them as reference when you talk with prospective companies.

Ask yourself:

- Why do I want to have a business of my own?
- What kind of work do I want? Part time? Full time? One party a month?
- How much money do I want to make, and am I willing to do what it takes to get there?
- Am I a goal-oriented person, and can I handle the ups and downs that the sex-toy party business can sometimes entail?
- Am I willing to make the financial investment required to buy the kit and purchase the things I need to have a successful business?
- Do I need a steady income to make ends meet?
- How will I market myself and get my parties started?
- Does the product the company offers meet my comfort level?
- Does the party company offer me support so I can have a more successful business?
- What kind of incentive program is offered for the work involved?

- Do I want to be a solo venture, or would I prefer to manage a line of reps working under me?

Some sex-toy party companies are structured in such a way that you will only make a decent income when you build a "down-line" (i.e., recruit other representatives underneath you). If your goal is a part-time income for part-time work, this is not a good structure for you because you will have constant pressure to recruit the next person in your down-line. A better setup for you is to sign on with a company that offers the most amount of money for your first-level sales.

Be honest about what you need, and what you expect from yourself. Depending on your financial situation, you may decide it is better to forego making money up-front in order to receive a large payout at the end. If you need a steady income to make ends meet, however, this is not a good structure for you. That's why you need to look honestly at why you are interested in this business and what your expectations for income are.

Ultimately, you want to find a company with the structure, support and compensation program that makes it the easiest for you to perform. Your ideal company will give you the least amount of work for the most amount of money (work = time).

EVALUATING START-UP COSTS

Unfortunately, nothing comes for free. Even as a representative for an established sex-toy party company, you will need to make some initial investments to get off the ground and get started throwing parties. The good news is, these expenses are not as big as if you were launching an independent business. Be aware of and realistic about these costs, however, so that you can figure out how much time and work will be required to earn back your initial investment...and begin making money!

There are three basic areas to consider when evaluating start-up costs: the cost of your kit, the cost of marketing materials and how long it will take to receive a return on your investment. You should also find out about any qualification conditions a company requires.

Kit Costs   All sex-toy party companies charge for the initial party kit. The cost of this kit—and the contents of it—can vary greatly. Although the basic party kit may be tempting because it's the cheapest option, we do not recommend it. You need to have enough products in your kit to be able to show a good variety at your first party. You also don't want customers to feel your offering is too limited. If you skimp on your first kit, your sales will suffer. Plan on making an initial investment of at least $400; this should get you set up with a nice choice of salesworthy products, order forms and basic marketing materials. (Note: If the company that you select requires you to carry inventory, don't forget to include these costs.)

Marketing Costs   You may have to dig a little deeper to discover any extra costs you will be expected to cover as a new rep. For example, do you need to buy your own business cards, product catalogs, invitations or hostess gifts? Average costs for these run around $100 to $200 for most party companies. Do you want to put an ad in the local paper? This can run you from $25 up. Will you be hosting the first party at your house? All of these are costs that quickly add up—so make sure to figure these into your start-up calculations.

Return on Investment This is the magical formula that makes a business successful. "Return on investment" can be defined simply as getting back more money than what you put in. To determine what it will take for you to receive a return on investment, you need to account for all your start-up costs and then compare them to the rate of income you expect to achieve. This will tell you how long it will take—how many parties with how many sales—for you to earn back your investment and start making money. Since different companies have different compensation structures, you'll want to figure out this formula for each company that you are considering. This is important to do *before* you commit to repping for a company. It could save you from making a costly mistake or committing to the wrong company.

When evaluating start-up costs, think of yourself as investing in your business. You want to make a good investment. If you put $5 in a savings account and then earn $5 more from interest, then you have received a return on investment of 100%. While all investors wish for this high rate of return, most returns on investment are in reality much smaller. The goal is simply to get more back than what you put in—this is your "break even point." It may take five parties, ten parties or just one party to break even, depending on the amount of your start-up costs and the sales rate at your parties.

To project accurately what your return on investment will be, you need to be realistic about the rate you expect to work and be clear about your company's compensation plan. If you only want to throw one party per month and you calculate that it will take approximately 12 parties to earn back the cost of your kit, you can then decide: are you willing to wait until the second year before you start making money? Probably not! Remember, when deciding which company is right for you, you need to approach this from a numbers perspective, not just an emotional one.

Qualification Conditions As you are investigating companies to rep for, check whether they have qualification and "staying active" provisions in their agreements. Staying qualified usually involves a certain dollar amount of merchandise that you must purchase from the company, or sell for the company (depending upon their structure) to maintain your status as an active representative. In most companies you must be qualified and stay active to participate in promotions, use their merchant account (if applicable) or purchase from the company—and to collect a percentage on sales from any representatives you recruited. If you let your status fall to inactive by not moving enough product, you may have to pay a fee to reactive yourself. Some companies also require an annual registration fee to remain active. Make sure to check this out before you sign up.

EVALUATING COMPENSATION PLANS

In this business, *how* you get paid can be as important as *how much* you get paid. There are two basic compensation plans. The first pays you through a percentage commission on sales made. The other is different; you earn money through the mark-up you charge on products you've purchased at wholesale cost. Companies that are structured on a commission basis, which is how Lady Bliss works, will generally take care of order fulfillment for you. Companies that pay through the mark-up method have their reps buy inventory and fulfill their own orders.

If you only look at the income received on orders, it may seem that you will break even faster with a mark-up based company, but if you factor in the time it takes you to place and fill orders that rate may be slower. The best way to evaluate this aspect of a sex-toy party business is to consider not only how much money you can make but also how much labor you need to put in to make every dollar. Look at both the compensation plan and the sales structure to get a complete picture.

Another way to earn income is by recruiting. In many companies you can earn a fee for recruiting new reps to the company or to your team. If your plan is to build a large distribution team and you want to have a number of reps under your wing, then look for a compensation plan that rewards initiative.

Most sex-toy party reps, however, do not want their compensation heavily dependent on recruiting. Even in a multi-level-oriented plan, most reps only recruit one or two people. Most people just don't have big enough networks to recruit more than that. If you have not made a career of sales and are not planning on building a huge team, look for a company that has incentives and benefits that will reward you for more than just recruiting; otherwise, you will probably never be happy.

EVALUATING SALES STRUCTURES

Now comes one of the most important evaluation areas of the sex-toy party business. You've considered start-up costs, compensation plans and recruiting. You've broken out your calculator, run your numbers and have a general idea of how to get a return on your initial investment. By now, you've probably found some companies that fit your personality and comfort level. What's left? Making the sale!

Which companies will make it easiest for you to make that sale? It depends on how much you want to work and how you prefer to spend your work time. It also depends on what your customers want, and what you can feasibly give them. Do you want to deliver the products to the hostess, or can your company mail them out? Do you want to be able to process your customers' credit cards? If so, this means obtaining a merchant bank account.

If you want to work only four to five hours per month, how is your time best spent? Stocking inventory, tracking how much product you have for the next party and shelling out your hard-earned cash to purchase more inventory? Of course not! You want to be booking, partying and selling your heart out. So look for a party plan that frees you up to do just that. If you want to take this on as a full-time business, then it might make more sense time- and money-wise to bite off the inventory and order fulfillment.

Fulfillment We're talking order fulfillment here, not sexual…although if you do your job right, the one will lead to the other!

Okay, so you've had your party, it was wonderful, you've taken orders and now it is time to fill them. Some companies will take each guest in a back room, take their order, hand them their brown paper bag full of goodies, and off the party guest goes—dildo and tasty treat in hand. This works well for many people. However, this system requires reps to stock inventory and haul it to the party. As a rep, you also need to forecast what the party guests are going to order and make sure you have enough inventory. If you run out, then you have to decide whether you will deliver the order to the hostess or the customer. All of this costs time and money.

Another fulfillment option is that you take the orders, go home and fill them, then drop them all off with the hostess for distribution. While this can also work well, the drawback to this method is that some partygoers may not feel comfortable with the hostess holding their order and perhaps

A NOTE ON CREDIT CARDS

When it comes to credit cards, let's be honest: most people prefer to deal with plastic, especially in direct sales. Credit cards give the customer a means for recourse if they're not happy with their purchases or do not receive the items they have ordered. To be successful in a direct sales company, you need to be able to take credit cards.

Although our business is not pornographic in nature, we are considered to be within the adult sex industry. Dealing with "adult products" can actually make it more difficult to obtain a merchant account. You may be required to give some type of deposit. In addition, as with any business, you will be required to pay transaction fees and a monthly processing fee—the amounts will vary by company. Transactions fees will be a percentage of the purchase (generally anywhere from 2.5 to 4.5 percent) in addition to a set amount (maybe $0.25) per transaction. (Note: Some party companies will set up the merchant account for you and then charge you a fee per transaction or a straight percentage. If you need to get your own merchant account, expect the costs to be much higher. Also, the deposit required may be based on your personal credit.)

discovering what they purchased. This is a private purchase and most people, no matter how outgoing and sex-positive, do not want the world to know they will be using the world's largest multi-speed thrusting 10-inch mechanism vibrator, glow-in-the-dark cock ring or ejaculation-delaying edible gel.

The last fulfillment option is to ship orders directly to the individual. The shipping can either be handled by the rep (which becomes an extra cost to you) or by the company itself.

As a rep, carrying inventory can be a hassle. Where do you stock the dildos if you have children at home? What if you live in a hot climate and you're always toting delicate products in your car? In either case, having a company that takes care of order fulfillment for you is a big bonus.

At Lady Bliss we take care of order fulfillment for a variety of reasons, but the main one is that we want all our customers to receive the same high-quality level of products and services. Whether they are shopping from our website, catalog or a sex-toy party representative, they experience uniformly professional customer service because it's being handled by our corporate office. No leaky lubes, crushed boxes or damaged dildos for Lady Bliss customers!

One side note to consider: Every once in a while, we hear about a rep who takes the orders, takes the money but doesn't deliver the products. This bad apple can spoil it for the rest of us. She gives her company and other reps in the area a bad name. So we suggest you partner with a company that has control over its reputation and customer service. In the long run, it is the level of customer service that keeps customers coming back.

Inventory Management Just a quick note about inventory management. If you are repping for a company that requires you to place orders for your products and deliver them to your customers, then you will need some type of inventory management system. Below are two separate ways to manage your inventory, depending on whether you deliver products at the party or ship them afterwards.

Fulfilling products at the party—Create an inventory sheet of all the products you carry and how many of each you will be bringing with you. As you fill each order, indicate the items(s) sold in the appropriate boxes on the inventory sheet. After you have filled the orders, subtract the number sold from the original number you had in stock to see how many you should have left. This should equal what you really do have left. If not, double check your math and your orders of each item sold. You cannot afford to lose products.

For example:

PRODUCT NAME	Items taken	order 1	order 2	order 3	order 4	items left
Tasty Powder	6	1		1		4
Love Lotion	5		1	1	1	2
Pink Vibe	9	1	1	1	1	5
Handcuffs	2			1		1

Shipping from home after the party—If you are taking the orders home and then placing an order with your sex-toy party company, you will want to create a spreadsheet that tells you exactly how much you need to order. This way, you will not be managing inventory in your home. The less inventory you keep, the lower your risk of damaging or losing inventory. Once you have completed the spreadsheet and placed the order, you can then use that form as your own internal purchase order. You will now have a record of what you have sold and what needs to be shipped.

For example:

ORDER NUMBER	Tasty Powder	Love Lotion	Pink Vibe	Hand-cuffs	Massage oil	Lube
0051	I		I			I
0052		I				
0053			I	I	I	I
Totals	I	I	2	I	I	2

However you choose to manage your inventory, you must create a method for keeping track of it. Lost, misplaced, damaged or stolen inventory will cut into your profits; you want to be able to keep every dollar that you make.

Customer Service and Returns No one wants an unhappy customer, least of all you. So what about that party guest whose vibrator breaks after a week of use? To keep her happy, do you need to replace it yourself or will your company? Does the customer send it back to the home office for a refund? If the company does not have a comprehensive return policy, and you as a rep are expected to deal with the cost of returns, then you might want to reconsider. Most sex toys are made overseas and they are not always of the highest quality. Women who shop from parties are paying a premium and expect high-quality merchandise. If something breaks and cannot be replaced for free or at a reduced cost, they will be unhappy. For a rep, happy customers equal referrals and repeat customers.

A Final Note...

We hope by now you have realized that deciding which company is best for you involves so much more than saying, "WOW, I really like their stuff!" There are many factors to consider before diving in. In addition to the numbers and logistics discussed in this chapter, you may also want to explore some of the less tangible things that make each company unique.

Sex-toy parties are taking place in living rooms from Seattle to St. Louis, from California to Kentucky. And new companies, large and small, are popping up everyday. Basically they all sell the same kinds of products. What makes the company you choose different from all the rest?

- The training of the reps
- The quality of the products
- The company's commitment to the customer
- How the products are distributed to the customer
- The company's popularity in your area

Lastly, before you make a commitment to the company of your dreams, check out the company's overall health. Have they been in business long? Have you heard good things about them? Is their brand familiar or popular? Is their compensation plan logical, or is it "too rich?" If they compensate significantly better than their competition, how long do you think they will be able to stay in business? There have been many party companies that launched with great fanfare, but then fizzled out because they were unable to re-main profitable. If you are building your business and making a name for yourself, you want the party company to grow stronger as well. If the company goes out of business in six months, this will hurt your momentum—and believe us when we tell you, building a sex-toy party business is all about momentum. Whether in sex or sex toys, this old adage still holds true: "If it sounds too good to be true, it probably is."

That said, where else can you start a business with start-up costs under $1000? Where else can you bring joy and romance to improve women's lives and relationships? If you're willing to work hard and take this on, there is beauty and satisfaction in this business!

SEVEN

Size Doesn't Matter: Starting Your Own Small Business

Starting your own business is a lot like giving birth and raising children. This new business will be your baby, with similar challenges and demands. Luckily, if your business fails you have not unleashed a maniac on society. You should expect to be emotionally tied to your business, because you will put lots of time and energy into making it successful. The challenges of the start-up are unique and different from running an established company. For both of us, Lady Bliss was not our first business venture so we came into it knowing what to expect. For those of you who are new to start-ups, here is an overview of the beginning challenges that you will face.

- The birth: What will you name your company?
- The birth certificate: What legal structure will choose? You will have legal paperwork to get in order, including bank accounts and business licenses.

- The costs of the birth: Where will the initial start-up funding come from—savings, your credit cards, a home equity loan, loans or gifts from relatives?
- The first-year plan: How are you going to run and market your business, who does what, whose talents can you readily tap and who do you need to hire?

The real challenge with any business is turning your ideas into action. Whether you are repping for an established company or starting your own sex-toy party business, implementation of ideas into actions is key—thinking is one thing and doing is another. The best part is when you begin to reap the rewards of your actions. When we first started the development of the Ladybliss.com website it seemed as if we would never be finished with the development and testing. We were so anxious for the site to "go live" to see how it would be received and whether people would actually order from us. We were so excited the day that our first orders were placed. Our actions had begun to bear fruit.

Owning your own company can be scary. The buck stops with you—if your company fails, there's no one else to blame. But there are also valuable benefits: You are your own boss and you can set the rules. You can do things your way, and your results will be based on your own talents.

Sisters Are Doing It for Themselves

The thought of starting your own business is an exciting but sometimes scary prospect. You may have hundreds of questions running through your head, from finding financing to arranging phone book listings. Depending on your level of expertise, you may or may not have the answers to these questions. Luckily, there are many resources you can turn to for business guidance and advice. For business drive, however, you have to look inward.

Not all individuals are cut out to be business owners. Before you set about launching your own company, you need to ask yourself and have a strong answer as to why you want to go into business for yourself. Consider why you want to do this on your own and not under the umbrella of a larger company. What do you want the results of your business endeavors to be? Can you realize them any other way?

There are five traits of successful business owners: determination, self-motivation, leadership, good communication skills and high tolerance for risk-taking. This is a wide and deep pool of talents. Do you possess all of these characteristics? And are you willing to put everything on the line for your new business? If you are not sure if this is you, then

TALES FROM LADY BLISS LIFE

Planning before you launch your business is critical, but it is also important to remember that your plan needs to be flexible. Lady Bliss began as an Internet-based retailer, then expanded into a direct mail catalog. We decided to branch out into home parties because our customers were asking for this. Believe it or not, home parties were never in our original plan. We listened to the marketplace, keeping an eye out for opportunity, and evaluated our business goals and business potential. Home parties were a natural extension for us. And now home parties are synonymous with Lady Bliss!

talk to the people who know you best—your family and friends. Ask them if they can see you in business for yourself. What do they see as your strengths for this business? What do they see as your weaknesses? This is valuable input to have, and it comes from individuals who care about you the most.

What Do You Need to Get Started?

So, you are bound and determined to be your own boss, eh? You've got a passion for stirring people's passions. You have drive and determination that will take you places. With success in your sights, you're willing to sacrifice to get there. Let's get started!

Not only are you going to need to make a financial investment to start your business, you will also need to commit a significant amount of your time. Starting a sex-toy party business is all about parties, so you need to be able to serve two to three parties a week. This is the average number of parties needed to start your revenues flowing.

In order to run the business part of your sex-toy party business effectively, you need to have the following available:

- **Cash** Yes, like all businesses, this one requires that you have some up-front cash you can use to pay for the next five items on this list—we estimate you'll need up to $7500 to get started. (See the chart on page 116 for more on the capital you'll need.) You also need to be able to go without a steady income for a period of time until you earn back this initial investment and start making money.

- **A home office** (even if it's a closet!) You need a space that you can devote to keeping all your paperwork, party kit, inventory and other business-related things. Ideally this is a place with a door you can close—a place free from the inquisitive eyes and messy hands of kids, dogs, housemates and husbands.
- **Business licenses** In addition to registering your DBA and registering for a Federal Tax ID Number, you will also need a reseller's license.
- **A good name** Brand identity is important for any business; you want to name your company something that people will remember.
- **Marketing materials** You will need business cards, invitations, price sheets, order forms and so forth. There are many software programs out there that can help you to develop and print these basic marketing materials. Once you start needing these in quantity, it is more cost effective to take them to a copy shop such as Kinko's.
- **Advertising** If you don't advertise, how will prospective customers know you're in business? Do your research to make sure your ad dollars are wisely spent. You want the most bang for your buck.
- **Bookkeeping** A basic software program such as QuickBooks, Peachtree or MYOB should meet your accounting needs. Just make sure that the software you select has inventory capabilities and, if you are not software savvy, a strong Help section and instruction book. Many community colleges offer classes on software programs. (See page 88 in Chapter 6 for more tips for bookkeeping.)

• **Commitment**   We can't stress this enough. Starting a business isn't something to be entered into lightly. You've got to be passionate and willing to work your butt off. It's important to map out concrete goals…and big dreams!

One other thing that we strongly recommend is to learn as much as you can about the "lay of the land." Really get to know your marketplace—which means getting intimate with your customers, knowing the general retail availability of the products and shopping your competition so that you can differentiate yourself. This is priceless knowledge that will help

JUST HOW MUCH CAPITAL DO I NEED?

This is the barebones money you should have ready to start. You should also be prepared to input more money as needed for the first year at least. Costs can vary widely from state to state and depending on what products you decide to carry. Also, the sky's the limit for advertising costs. Below are some ballpark figures for basic expenses:

Business Licenses & Registrations	$ 200–$500
Product Inventory	$2000–$5000
Marketing Materials	$1000
Advertising (Initial)	$1000
TOTAL	up to $7500

you make good decisions. It can save you money, time and endless guessing and worrying. Good businesswomen develop their "chops" by hostessing and/or repping for a variety companies, interviewing other reps and engaging anyone they can in the industry (such as distributors, marketers and retailers).

The more you look for market research opportunities, the more you will realize that they are all around you. From learning about favorite sex toys over lunch with friends, to talking about the latest hot-selling panties with the clerk at Victoria's Secret, everyone's got insight into what can make your business successful. The trick is for you to put the right pieces together.

Building Your Product Line

What's a sex-toy party business without the sex and the toys? Nothing! Building your product line is not only fun, it is the foundation of your business. So make sure you do your research well before deciding which products you would like to carry. We suggest you begin by checking out the product lines of the larger sex-toy party companies. Book a few parties of your own with different companies so you can determine what you like and don't like—and so you can gauge the interest of the people who will be your future customers. (For more information on understanding your market, check out Chapter 3. For more detailed information on products, check out the product comparisons in Part Four.)

Do your research up front, but remember that there are several large distributors where you will be able to get everything that you need to cater to the needs of your clients.

Distributors: The Source of All Good Things

A distributor is the middleman between the sex-toy manu-facturers and you. Finding a distributor that is located close to you will help, since you will be required to pay the cost of the products getting to you. If you are in New York, you want to find an East Coast distributor if possible. If you're located in Los Angeles, look for distributors in the Pacific Northwest or Nevada.

We recommend using only two distributors, with the second distributor as your backup. This way you can keep things streamlined, develop ongoing deeper business relation-ships and receive better pricing. Distributors give greater dis-counts if you order in quantity from them, so limiting the number of companies you order from will increase your margins. Use the second distributor in case your primary distributor is out of stock or doesn't carry some products you want. Ideally, you should be able to get at least 95 per-cent of your product line from both distributors.

When shopping for distributors, ask them to send you their product catalogs and price lists. Also make sure to find out about their ordering, shipping, backorder and return policies. We have dealt with distributors in the past that do not notify you when items are on backorder, instead they just don't ship. This can be frustrating when you have cus-tomers waiting for products.

Once you've identified your distributors, you will set up what's called a vendor-supplier relationship with them. They will require you to pay for your orders up front or open an account with them (in which case you need to prove you have credit). You will purchase your products from them at a wholesale price, which is a significant discount off the retail price at which you will sell the products (approximately 60 to 80 percent off of the retail price). You make your money by reselling the products to your customers at retail price. The money you make, or your "profit margin," is the difference between the two. In the sex-toy party business you should be looking to make at least a 40 percent margin on your products. Remember: you will be giving away some percentage to your hostesses. If you have reps then you will want an even greater margin as you will also have to give a percentage away to them. Your pricing needs to be set so that you can make money but still stay competitive. Shop your competition to see what their prices average.

In addition to supplying your product, distributors can also be great business resources. If you develop a good working relationship with them, they can tell you valuable infor-

TALES FROM LADY BLISS LIFE

When we started out with Ladybliss.com we had only three major suppliers and an initial product line of approximately 320 products. When we started the home parties we had to choose only 60 products for our party kits. This was so hard to do! We love all the products that we carry on the website and hated to eliminate any of them from our party offering. But carrying more than 60 would have been overwhelming and impractical. So we decided that our reps just needed websites of their own. That's creative thinking.

mation about the business. They can alert you to new products coming onto the market, let you in on which products are their top-sellers, and may even have the inside scoop on upcoming trends in your marketplace.

See Chapter 19 for more information on distributors, including contact information for some of our favorites.

Challenges to Watch Out For

The toughest challenges that you will face as an independent business owner are marketing your company and keeping a fresh and strong product line. These two issues, not surprisingly, will also be instrumental in your success. The reason that marketing and maintaining the product line can be so difficult is that they are time-consuming and can make or break your business.

MARKETING

If your marketing fails your bookings will not grow, or worse, they may dry up. If sales die down, you will run out of cash. Once you loose momentum in a business, it is even harder to recapitalize and motivate yourself to start again. Marketing can be tough as it is time-consuming and may or may not yield your desired results. A good way to tackle your marketing is to make a list of three things that you will do every day to increase the growth of your business and directly add to your bottom line.

For example:

- Follow up with hostesses who had parties between January 1 and February 29th and see if I can get any referrals or new party bookings.

- Contact local salons and see if I can leave some business cards on their counter.
- Review local newspapers for advertising ideas.

If you can consistently do something daily to increase sales, your business will grow.

KEEPING YOUR OFFERINGS FRESH

If your product line does not stay fresh and new, people may begin to shop your competition. Or, they may see a need to create your competition and start their own company. Keep in mind that women talk and they will bump into individuals who have attended parties hosted by your competitors. If your competition is constantly upgrading with new toys that are getting some buzz in magazines then you could start to lose out to them. Remember that your customers are individuals who are exploring their sexuality and they will want to try new gizmos. So keeping the product line exciting is imperative and takes work but is worth it.

INVENTORY MANAGEMENT

This is also a big challenge for many businesses. You must be very detailed with your inventory controls so that you know what you have at all time. You can't afford for items to "walk away" at parties, get lost or be sold at a loss. When margins and sales are small, having one expensive vibrator stolen can be a financial setback. Some key tips for inventory management are:

- Make an investment in software that has inventory capabilities.
- Create a purchase order for each order that you place.

- Match the items that are delivered to your purchase order to make sure that you received what you ordered. Also match your purchase order to the invoice or sales receipt to make sure that you were charged correctly.
- Record all sales on a sales receipt.
- Record all damaged goods that you remove from the inventory.
- Record all free gifts, prizes, etc. that you remove from the inventory.
- Print out an ending inventory report at the end of each month. This should show all the ins and outs of your inventory and give you a final count for each inventory item.
- Count your inventory and compare it to your calculated form. If your inventory controls are working, these numbers should match.

Inventory management is a must but doesn't have to be hard. There are plenty of software packages on the market that will make managing your inventory a breeze. Both QuickBooks (www.quickbooks.com) and Peachtree (www.peachtree.com) as well as MYOB (www.myob.com) have inventory packages built into their accounting so you can do your bookkeeping and manage your inventory at the same time. However, some of these packages will not offer multiple pricing tiers.

BAD DEBT

Unfortunately, you must be wary of customers' declined credit cards and bounced checks. One of the benefits of not carry-

FIVE COMMON MISTAKES OF START-UPS

There are five common mistakes and pitfalls of start-ups:

1. Failing to obtain adequate capitalization and credit reserves.
2. Failing to create a detailed marketing plan and to measure marketing outcomes, therefore wasting money on ineffective marketing.
3. Failing to give marketing enough time to have an effect on customers. Most consumers need to see things multiple times before they act on it.
4. Failing to have adequate controls in place for inventory and cash management.
5. Failing to realize the importance of superior customer service, and losing repeat business as a result.

ing products to parties for immediate order fulfillment is that you do not have to worry about this. If a check bounces or a credit card is rejected, you don't have to fill the order. Filling orders after the party gives you time to validate the credit card, and if there is a problem, gives the customer an opportunity to make it right with you. Always get a phone number when you accept a personal check, but understand that collecting on bad checks can be difficult at best and laws vary by state as to how far you can go with collection efforts. Besides cash, credit cards are the safest way to guarantee payment. But make sure to have your customers sign a credit card receipt whenever possible. This gives you signed documentation to mail to the credit card company if the customer for some reason disputes the charge.

Ultimately, It's All about Sales

Before you actually launch your own business, think honestly about whether you really like the product line and whether you're *really* into selling sex toys. Imagine investing a significant amount of money and then discovering that you actually hate it. We have met many women who pay $600 for a sex-toy party rep kit and then do nothing with it. We have also met women who started their own party companies and invested a great amount of capital, only to discover that the time commitment is larger than they originally thought and they want out.

When Lady Bliss launched home parties, we had a rep who was absolutely gung ho over sex toys. In fact, she is the primary reason we launched the home parties in the first place. She had used sex toys and accoutrements for years, they were integral to her life, and she really enjoyed spreading the word about their wonders in the boudoir. At the time we were actually quite happy being an Internet company, but this woman wanted to sell our product line in homes so we said okay, we'll give it a try. After her second party she didn't want to rep any more. It was too much work for her, despite having spent over $700 on her kit, gifts and marketing materials.

When you get into this business you have to understand from the very beginning, sex-toy parties are *work*. Sometimes sales can be disappointing. Yes, guests at your parties will be drinking, laughing and having fun—and you will have fun too—but the bottom line is that you are there to sell, not to party. And depending on the party, selling can include education, show-and-tell, crowd control and whatever it takes to get your customers excited and interested in buying your products. Before you start your own business, take the time to rep for another company first to make sure that this is what you want to do. Trust us, before you dive in, make sure you want to do it from the bottom of your heart and the sole of your shoes.

If, at the end of the day, you are an independent, risk-taking, self-motivating individual who is planning on doing two to three parties a week and has the time, the money and the passion to commit to launching a sex-toy party business, then you have the potential to earn more money in the long run as an independent businesswoman than as a rep for another company. Keep in mind that this path also means you will invest your time, effort and money on the front end, but that you will not see a return on this effort and money until much later down the road.

There are definitely some upsides to running your own company and one if them is that you have control—control over how your message is delivered, the product line you offer, your customer service and your pricing. But there is also an increased amount of responsibility that accompanies control. You are taking a much greater risk with time and money, but your potential outcome—increased wealth, satisfaction and independence—is why you are taking this kind of risk.

So, to wrap up: Are you ready and willing to go it alone? If you think that you are going to host at least two to three parties a week, have approximately $7500 that you can invest in your own business and have the time and energy to grow a new company, then starting your own sex-toy party business may indeed be for you.

EIGHT

Sex-Toy Tycoon: Dream Big—Grow Large!

This section is for those of you with big dreams and ambition to match. Do you hope someday to run a company like the ones we discussed repping for? Do you want to grow a large company with a sizable base (200-plus reps) from the ground up? The basics of this type of business are the same as any sex-toy party business, but they take on a much grander scale. Building a big business requires more cash, more paperwork, more preparation, more sweat and tears, more payoff...and yes, a good lawyer too!

What Is Your Vision?

It's especially important for a large company to have a clear focus. You need to pick a vision and stick to it. At each step of the way, from planning your business to implementing it, you must keep your vision in the forefront of your mind, because others will try to influence or change your vision. Your vision is your unchanging ideals and should not be influenced by industry structure or by products. Once you have your vision, then you put these ideals into words and create your company's mission statement.

The Lady Bliss mission statement is: "**The Definition of Bliss: A State of Euphoria and Being in a Complete State of Happiness**—Our company is committed to celebrating and enhancing this state of being by offering women from all walks of life a way to elevate and explore their romantic lives and individual sexuality in a safe and enriching online and offline environment."

Your company's vision is created from your ideals; your mission statement is just putting those ideals into words that

---

TALES FROM LADY BLISS LIFE

As we were launching Lady Bliss Home Parties, we attended a convention regarding direct sales and heard from a speaker discussing mission statements. She had founded a company that created and packaged easy-to-make mixes for family dinners. Her vision was to make it possible for busy families to have time to sit around the dinner table and enjoy each other, and this was conveyed in the company mission statement. One evening when the company was in the midst of a growth spurt, she noticed how many of her employees were working well after 7 p.m. She had this beautiful vision of families eating together, but she was not implementing this vision within her own company. She realized she needed to make changes.

you can follow. For example, "My sex-toy party company will be open to all women of all races and origins by providing them with a method to achieve financial independence" is an ideal put into words, thus creating a mission statement. To figure out what you intend your vision to be involves asking yourself some questions about what you want to accomplish.

Ask yourself:

- What are my core values?
- What is my core purpose?
- What are my visionary goals?

Now, if you reread the mission statements of Lady Bliss and Homemade Gourmet, you can see how these mission statements answer these questions. You will want to keep your mission statement where you and your employees can read it regularly.

Once you have identified your vision and written down your mission statement, you are ready to address all the other start-up needs: money, goal setting, time frames, drive and determination and the ability to pick yourself up and go again.

Get a Good Lawyer!

As a company bent on growth, your legal needs become complicated: Once you start to have reps, you need a legal agreement with them. When you start to do business in other states, you need to worry about their laws and taxes. So, if you are starting down the path of sex-toy tycoon, our first suggestion is to find yourself a good, solid business lawyer who can give you all the information you need to get started on the right foot. "A lawyer?" you may be saying. "Are you sure about this? What is the worst that could happen if I don't consult a lawyer?" Picture this: You have just opened your doors for business. You sign your first rep, and in one month you have five more. You never had an official rep agreement, or maybe you wrote up something yourself, and suddenly you're faced with a calamitous legal issue. One of your reps talks the others into leaving and joining another company. Your business is gone in the blink of an eye. Why? Because you didn't take the time to have your rep agreement reviewed by a lawyer to ensure it was legally binding. "But what if my reps are my friends?" you say. All the more reason to put your business relationship in writing. When you have a contract, the law takes care of your professional obligations so that your friendship never has to.

When looking for a lawyer you need to figure out what your business needs are. Do you need an agreement? Do you need a legal opinion on something? Then you want to find a lawyer who specializes in that area. Ask your family and friends or business associates for a referral. If that doesn't pan out, then ask other professionals you may know, such as a banker or an accountant. You may also want to use a lawyer referral service. Once you have created a list of lawyers, you will want to set up a phone interview to narrow down the list. Ask questions such as:

• How long have you been in practice?
• How much experience do you have in XYZ?

- Is this a standard issue with a standard fee or do you charge by the hour?
- Do you charge for your initial consultation?

You want to find someone who is knowledgeable, but whose rates you can afford. It helps to find someone you can get along with, as you may want to maintain a long-term relationship.

We also recommend you do some research on your own—and pick up some fun bedtime reading!—with Nolo Press (www.nolo.com). They have excellent online publications as well as books about legal issues for business owners and especially do-it-yourselfers.

Mapping the Path from Businesswoman to Sex-Toy Tycoon

In addition to everything we discussed in Chapter 7 on starting your own small business, you will face extra dreaming, planning and investment issues. We cannot stress enough how important planning is to your business even if your plan changes multiple times. It is not unusual for the planning process to take at least six months or longer. That said, take care that you don't get caught in what is called "analysis paralysis"—where you spend all your time planning and none of your time doing. What follows are some of the major areas where you will want to focus your planning efforts. Once you have solid plans in place, move forward toward implementation.

Business Plan   For a larger company, you definitely want to put together a business plan. It doesn't need to be elaborate, but it should be the place where you write down your future plans for your business and your marketing strategies. A typical business plan includes your expectations for initial costs and investment, cash flow, ongoing expenditures, marketing and sales. It should cover plans for one to three years. Your business plan should be revisited at least quarterly or whenever you make a significant change in direction, such as moving your focus to a new hot sales segment. Believe us, your business plan will change and grow, just like a child, because with experience and time things change. It is important, however, that you put your first vision for your company down on paper, and in detail. This is how you will measure where you have been, and how you will modify where you are going with your business. There are lots of classes, books and other resources out there to help you with business planning. The website www.businessplans.org is a good place to start.

Rep Plan Part of your planning process will be to determine the structure for your reps. After all, they are the building blocks of your business. Your rep plan should include: your goals for growing the rep portion of your business, compensation structure, how you plan on incorporating new products, communication with your reps, motivators and promotions. It should also cover issues that affect reps, such as shipping, customer service policies, dissatisfied customers and returns. For instance, you come back from a new product trade show and want to have your reps carry some of the new products you saw there. Do you give samples to them? Offer the products at a special discount? What happens if a rep has a customer whose toy breaks the first day of use? Does the rep take care of this customer and get her a new product or does the main office handle it? And who pays for the broken products?

Training Plan   To build a successful fleet of reps, you need consistent, dedicated, educated, customer service-oriented people. And then you need a good training plan. You can't just throw women out there and expect them to be able to sell your products. You need to support them, so they can support you. Your brand, your vision, and your sales reps are an extension of your business, so you need to be clear about what they know, what they do, and what you want from them. Some companies offer in-person training through training seminars. Others send a three-ring binder full of policies and procedures, and yet others send a training video. The method in which you train your reps will probably change as your business grows; your in-person time may become more precious, your procedures may become more standardized, and some of these methods may become less cost-prohibitive.

Financial Plan   Since starting and growing a large business requires more capital, increases expenditures, and (with luck) earns you more income, your finances will be more complicated. It is critical that you plan them out carefully so that you have a guide to follow. If this is not your area of expertise, then pulling in a part-time financial consultant may be your best bet. This will increase your initial expenditures, but it will also ensure that you are set on the correct path from day one. A financial consultant will make sure that the proper controls are in place, that your inventory system works smoothly, and that proper banking relationships are set up and working. A good financial consultant can also support you in dealing with a business attorney. You should also expect to spend financial resources on figuring out a compensation plan, creating marketing materials, designing and building a website, developing training resources and building product lines A financial plan is not a substitute for an operating budget (you'll need one of those, too!), but it can serve as the baseline for one. An operating budget is what you will compare your financial results to; a financial plan is your guide.

Great Expectations

Sex-toy tycoons are like Girl Scouts: always prepared! Don't jump in head first without first measuring how deep the water is. Dream big, aim high, but also develop realistic expectations for....

Time Growing your business into an empire doesn't happen overnight. If Rome wasn't conquered in a day, you can't expect to place a sex toy in every woman's bedroom in a short time frame, either. Remember that successful growth is a slow and steady endeavor. It will happen over months and years, not days and weeks.

Competition Competition is a good thing. Never look at it as a negative. Competitors allow the word of what you do to spread even more. What you will need to do is study your competition and figure out what you do differently and what differentiates your business from theirs. This differentiation is one of your selling points. Think about your competition critically in terms of who they are targeting, what they do well, and their strengths and weaknesses. Then apply these same questions to your company. Stay in touch with the developments of your competition, no matter how big you get. There is much to learn from competitors.

Making Money You cannot expect to get a half-million dollar return on a $2000 investment. You can expect, however, a half-million dollar return on a $50,000 investment if you run your business correctly. The good news is, you may not need to put in all the money up front—although your up-front costs will be substantial. Just don't plan on making any money for yourself for quite a while. Most of the revenue generated by your company will need to be put back into the company for marketing and inventory.

Investing More Money Once you launch your business, don't expect that your financial investment is complete. You will most likely need to make additional investments at critical periods of growth. Businesses run in sales cycles and although you can mitigate some of the risks through proper planning, you can never account for all of them. So expect to put more money in at some point down the road, and have these cash reserves available. If you don't have reserve cash on hand, set up some lines of credit with the bank. (And don't dip into these lines on whim or impulse! Use them for necessity, as contingency, or for calculated expansion.)

Challenges to Watch Out For

Advertising When it comes to advertising, it pays to do your research. Advertising can be a great way to gain customers and build brand recognition, but you need to move carefully, since advertising dollars are easily wasted. Before even thinking about placing an ad, make sure that you have a way to track phone calls or web hits inspired by the ad, so that you will know if your advertising is converting people to action. You may want to use a separate phone number or web address to keep track. We recommend that you do not advertise in the same media as your competitors unless you can go against them dollar for dollar. In your ads use testimonials from happy customers if at all possible, do not promise what you cannot deliver, and try to refer to things that would be familiar your target customer. For sex-toy party businesses, localized advertising works well. Remember, women need to be able to find you in order to book their parties.

Overhead The toughest part about overhead is that it is a fixed monthly expense. Just like your home mortgage or rent, overhead costs need to be paid every month, regardless of whether you are making money or not. High overhead costs can be extremely difficult for start-up companies, which is why there is such a high failure rate for businesses in their first two years. Not only do marketing and operations cost large amounts of money in themselves, you will need a staff of people to do any of these well. All are necessary if you want to build a successful company, but they do not need to break the bank. There are many ways to be frugal. Be warned about signing any long-term commitments and try to sublease space at first if possible. Look for businesses that are closing and buy their used furniture and office equipment. You want your overhead to grow as your business grows; you don't want to burden yourself with high overhead costs from day one.

Keeping Tabs on the Numbers When a business starts to grow quickly, owners and employees are often stretched and overburdened. At these times, it is not uncommon for things to begin to slip through the cracks, including financial items. To avoid the costs of problems that can arise from this, make sure that someone is always watching your numbers. Implement reporting as soon as it becomes available so that you can hold individuals accountable for their income and expenses. Many businesses struggle because someone thought someone else was covering a needed task, and they weren't. Make it a company priority to keep communications open.

Hiring and Retaining Staff Once you get to the point where you are hiring employees, you need to consult a human resources expert. In all industries sexual harassment needs to be carefully addressed, but when you have employees packing dildos it can take on a whole new meaning! You will need to create an employee manual, understand the labor laws and figure out how you plan on compensating and retaining employees. A good human resources consultant can help.

A Final Note

You need to start small and grow large, but always keep your eyes on the prize. It is a delicate balance between responding to the current state of your company while actively focusing on your long-term ultimate goal: sex-toy tycoon! You go, girl.

PART FOUR

What's the Buzz? Erotic Product Profiles

Now that you have an understanding of who your customer is and what her needs and desires are, it's time to get down and get dirty with your products. Knowing the ins and outs of your product line—literally!—is the single most important part of your sex-toy party business. At most parties, you will be working with some women who have little or no experience with sensual products. They will be relying on you to guide them. If you are not comfortable with your products, don't know how they work and can't offer ideas about how to use and incorporate erotic products into lovemaking, you will not be successful at selling them.

In this section, we give you the lowdown on the variety of products out there, from A to V. (From anal beads to vibrators, that is!) This will help you determine which lines of products are right for your market, select the best ones for your kit and become a confident, educated, successful party presenter. We have also provided you with contact information to look into purchasing your products, either from the manufacturer or from a distributor. But be aware that you need to be in business before contacting distributors; they don't just sell to anyone off the street.

You can never know too much about sex toys when you are in the sex-toy business—so read, read and then read some more. A great book to buy for more toy education is Sadie Allison's *ToyGasms! The Insider's Guide to Sex Toys and Techniques.* This book will give you tons of information on how to describe to your customers the uses of sex toys and other products. We have actually used some of her suggested techniques in our party presentations when talking about the sex toys we carry. Consider including it in your kit, so that your customers can benefit from Sadie's knowledge as well.

The world of sex toys is a big one, with literally hundreds of products made to fit every type of sensual need. New products come out on a regular basis and some are inevitably discontinued. So the biggest challenge for every sex-toy party representative is to select a wide variety of products that are not only of the highest quality, but the best selling as well. That is why it is so important to understand your market and the types of products that will best suit their tastes.

One last word of advice before you choose any products for your kit: make sure you request a catalog from your prospective distributors and manufacturers. (Or if you are

HOW TO BUY

Should you buy all your products from a distributor, or buy some directly from the manufacturer when you can? Buying direct cuts out the middleman, allowing you to make more profit off those products. However, manufacturers may require minimum buys, which may make buying from a distributor more cost effective because they usually have no minimums, or very low ones, helping to lower your costs as you are growing your business. See Chapter 19 for more on our favorite suppliers.

repping for a sex-toy party company, request their catalog.) This way you can check out the products and the packaging. At Lady Bliss we are particular about the packaging of our products because we don't want our customers to be offended by anything pornographic on the box. We carry many Top-Cat Products because they not only manufacture quality products, but provide beautiful packaging with no nudity. We have done our best to recommend products that have tasteful packaging, but this is not always possible since some manufacturers still haven't caught on to the fact that women don't like looking at a naked porn star when buying toys for themselves or a partner. However, having said that, there are many popular and quality products that have some kind of nudity on the packaging, so it comes down to you knowing your market and what your customers will be comfortable buying. If you are repping for a sex-toy party company, beware if they tell you to remove the product from the packaging if you find it offensive. We have had manufacturers actually recommend that we do this, which tells us other party companies must be doing this. But the package is what keeps a product clean and in good condition. Who wants to buy a sex toy that's not clean? Yuck!

NINE

Dildos

Dildos are non-vibrating toys that come in a rainbow of colors, shapes and sizes. If it goes buzz, it's not a dildo. Dildos can have the appearance and feel of a real penis, or they can bear no resemblance to male anatomy. They can look like a big, purple jelly phallus complete with balls, like a lovely dolphin or like a shiny bullet. They can be used for vaginal or anal penetration. Some dildos are specially shaped to get at that glorious G-spot, and some come with suction cups on the bottom so you can stick them to surfaces. They are an easy introduction to the wonderful world of toys for the first-timer or the tentative sex-toy user.

Dildos are easy to use because you control the stroking motion and they allow for creativity: stroke them outside the vagina to pleasure the clitoris and massage the labia, or use internally to stimulate the vagina while using a finger to massage the clitoris. You can use a vibrator and dildo together, massaging the clitoris with the vibrator while stroking inside with the dildo or vice-versa. Many couples like dildos for fore-

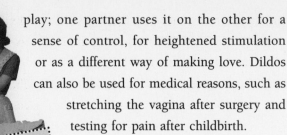

play; one partner uses it on the other for a sense of control, for heightened stimulation or as a different way of making love. Dildos can also be used for medical reasons, such as stretching the vagina after surgery and testing for pain after childbirth.

However dildos are used, they are sure to bring lots of pleasure! Dildos are made of many different types of material. Here is a quick look at some of the most popular...

Silicone Dildos

These dildos are usually of the highest quality and often cost more than other varieties. They feel like the real deal and they retain heat so the experience is that much more enjoyable. They are hypoallergenic, non-porous and easy to clean. You can boil them in water or even stick them on the top rack of your dishwasher!

Our favorite silicone dildos are made by Tantus. The Tantus Techno hits the G-spot, and the Echo, which is in the shape of a spiral, has an unusual titillating feel. Made in the United States (which is unusual as most toys are made overseas), the Tantus dildos come in beautiful feminine colors,

SALES TIPS: DILDOS

These fabulous toys generally do not sell themselves, so you must explain their sexy and practical uses. Describe all the benefits these flexible gadgets offer. Relay stories you've heard from creative satisfied users and encourage your customers to imagine how they could use these products.

are harness compatible, and have a separate vibrator for the times you feel like getting your buzz on! You can find them at www.tantussilicone.com.

We also recommend Top Cat's Neo-Jel collection. They come not only in beautiful colors but in a variety of shapes and sizes as well. One of our favorites is the 7-inch Neo-Jel Dong with Suction Cup. You can find Top Cat products at www.americanlatex.com.

A smaller California company that makes wonderful silicone products is Vibratex. They use only the best materials and their products clearly reflect that. One of their nicer silicone dildos is the Dildorine, which is also harness compatible. You can contact them at 800-222-3361.

Jelly Dildos

Available in many fun sizes and shapes, jelly dildos feel really comfortable because they are usually pretty flexible. They also tend to be more affordable than some of the other dildos in the marketplace, jellies are made of porous material, so make sure you instruct women at your parties to wash their jelly dongs well!

Believe it or not, one of the most popular sellers at Lady Bliss is our purple jelly dong with suction cup and balls, which we affectionately call "Barney." Our motto: "Stick him here, stick him there, stick him everywhere. On the door, on the shower floor, he will make you want it more!" He has all kinds of fabulous uses! You can find him at www. americanlatex.com.

Supercocks by Benwa are soft and comfortable jelly dildos that come in an array of attractive colors and sizes that will do the trick just right. You can find them at www.benwa.com.

Top Cat's 7-Inch Jelly Dong with Clit Tickler can be quite delightful. You can find this at www.americanlatex.com.

"Looks and Feels Real" Dildos

These lifelike dildos are soft and feel like a real penis. They are usually not as hard as jelly or silicone dildos and are ideal for women who prefer something that simulates the real deal. Because they are made out of a soft, porous material they need special care. Give customers the following instructions: Keep these dildos extra clean to keep the germs away. Also, these types of dildos should be stored in a cool dry place away from other toys, as the material can break down and get sticky and gummy. Storing these with a dusting of hypoallergenic powder will help prevent this from happening and prolong their life span. Be sure to check periodically for cracks that can harbor bacteria. When cracks occur, it's definitely time to replace them. Tell your customers the texture of these is worth every penny, and keep them coming back to you for their replacements!

One of our top-selling "looks and feels real" dildos is our 7-inch Dong with Soft Balls, which is made with stretchy and soft NeoSkin silicone by Top Cat. They come in a variety of "flesh" colors, including cinnamon, cream and ebony. If you closed your eyes and touched it you would never know you weren't feeling the real thing. This dildo caused the now-famous "Shana Incident," when a man at a lingerie show shoved this in Shana's hand and almost caused her to run for the door because she thought someone was putting his penis in her hand. You can find them at www.americanlatex.com.

Other popular "looks and feels real" dildos are from Topco's line of Pleasureskin products. If you are into big dongs then you will love their 10-inch Super Dong, which has squeezable testicles. Believe it or not, you might get requests for something this large! (They also come in other sizes.) Topco is one of the largest manufacturers of adult toys in the United States. You can find them at www.topco-sales.com.

The Penthouse brand Cyberskin Extreme Cock with suction cup is a popular "looks and feels real" dildo that makes you forget you don't have him right next to you. You can find this and other "looks and feels real" Cyberskin dildos at www.topco-sales.com.

Acrylic Dildos

These dildos are hard, inflexible and made from non-porous materials, making them easy to keep clean. If you have women at your parties who like it hard, want an easy way to find their G-spot, or like anal play, this may be the type of dildo they prefer.

The Acrylic Crystal Wand by Nector Products is sensually curved to hit all the right spots. You can find this at Entrenue, 800-368-7268.

A really creative acrylic dildo is the 7.75-inch Ribbed Wand made by Holiday Products. It has a pleasure-driven contoured head with a long handle for easy use. You can buy this at www.holidayproducts.com.

Another interesting acrylic dildo is the Smooth Wand. With a smooth yet thin head and thicker body, it can be used for both vaginal and anal play. You can find this at www.holi dayproducts.com.

Glass Dildos

Glass you say? Yes, believe it or not! Glass dildos can be described as erotic pieces of art, with many beautiful colors, shapes and sizes available.  They are not only safe to use, non-porous, and easy to keep clean but you can even put them in the dishwasher. Another neat feature of these toys is that they can be heated or put in the freezer for different types of sensations. Glass dildos are truly a specialty item and are usually more costly than other toys. Make sure your market wants this type of dildo before you make the investment.

The Heart-On Glass Dong has a heart that you can use as a handle and a thick wand to use on all your favorite parts. There is one for vaginal use, one designed to hit the G-spot and one for anal use. You can find these at www.holi dayproducts.com.

One of our favorite manufacturers of glass dildos is Phallix. They make beautiful products and were one of the originals in the marketplace. Their toys are so beautiful that you almost hate to use them because it seems like they should go on a mantle or coffee table. One of their top sellers is called the Juicer. You can find them at www.phallix glass.com

E-Glass has become popular of late. The Spiral looks promising with seven inches of glass and spiral-ribbed ecstasy. These products are now being manufactured by Topco Sales. You can find them at www.holidayproducts.com.

Latex Dildos

While these dildos are not as lifelike and hard as silicone dildos, they do the job just fine. The downside to latex dildos is that some women can be prone to allergic reactions from this type of material. Latex dildos are porous, so they need extra cleaning after use. Without proper cleaning, their porous surface will harbor germs. At Lady Bliss we don't carry latex dildos because of the risk many women have of getting some sort of infection. With all of the new materials that adult toys are made of these days, we suggest that you not carry something that may have potential problems. Also, latex dildos tend to be less expensive and not as well made. However, we wanted to give you information on latex dildos because you will find them out in the marketplace and some people prefer latex over sex toys made with other materials.

TEN

Vibrators & Massagers

These are defined as any device that has an electrical or mechanical movement designed to arouse or soothe. They come in many shapes, colors, sizes and vibrating modes. Vibrators introduce a whole new type of erotic pleasure into the bedroom, and they can be used for clitoral, labial, vaginal, perineal and anal pleasures. At Lady Bliss we always encourage our customers to experiment with vibrators, both alone and with their partners. They add an exciting new dimension to making love.

There are many different types of vibrators. Here are some distinctions:

Jelly Vibrators

These vibrators come in many fun sizes and shapes, just like the jelly dildos. They also feel really good and often look like the real thing, only in color

and with veins and bumps to add a certain amount of stimulation. They are usually a little more affordable than some of the dual action jellies that you find in the marketplace. Jelly vibrators are made of porous material, so make sure you instruct your customers to wash their jelly vibrators well!

One of our favorite jelly vibrators is the Angel Vibe by Benwa. The packaging is not only beautiful and feminine; it's made of iridescent pink jelly, with a powerful vibrator throughout the whole shaft. Its dual controls are located on the bottom of the shaft, and it's as quiet as a mouse for those who need extra discretion. This is a must-have toy! You can find this at www.benwa.com.

Another great jelly vibrator is Top Cat's seven-inch Powerful, Multi-Speed Vibrating Studded Jelly Dong. The pleasure studs along the shaft offer you extra stimulation for a jelly of a good time. You can find this at www.american latex.com.

Last but certainly not least is Top Cat's seven-inch Powerful, Multi-Speed Vibrating Jelly Dong with Suction Cup. You can stick it here, there and everywhere for jelly vibrating fun. You can find this at www.americanlatex.com.

Hand Wands and Massagers

The most popular and recognizable toys available, these can be used not only for massage but as sex toys, and consumers can buy them at select retailers. They are very powerful and offer intense vibration, so tell your customers to use these toys over their underwear or with a towel over their clitoris to avoid overstimulating or hurting themselves. Hand wands and massagers usually can be plugged in or used cordless for unfettered fun.

The Acuvibe Massager has a rechargeable NiCad battery and can be used cordless for up to 45 minutes. The Hitachi Magic Wand plugs in and has attachments to enhance pleasure, which can be bought separately. These two toys cannot be bought directly from the manufacturer, so you must go through a distributor. You can order these from one of our favorite distributors, Entrenue. To receive a catalog or find out how to be one of their vendors, contact Entrenue at 800-368-7268.

The Wahl Massager is a top-quality and powerful hand massager. It comes with seven attachments to take care of every part of the body. You can buy this through Entrenue at 800-368-7268.

Benwa has their own versions of the Hitachi and Acuvibe massager in their Magic Massager Ribbed Wand and their Rechargeable Massager Wand. Contact them online at www.benwa.com.

SALES TIPS: VIBRATORS

Turn on your vibrators and let party guests feel them. Vibrators need to be touched to be sold. (Do not, however, offer to demonstrate or let others test them!) When showcasing vibrating bullets, offer some ideas on how to use them: alone, with a partner, for foreplay in the bedroom, in the shower, in an airplane bathroom during long flights...you get the picture! These little babies are discreet and can travel anywhere.

The Fukuoku Five Finger Fantasy is a waterproof, multi-speed massage glove that you can use on dry land as well. It vibrates at approximately 45,000 vibes per minute, for about an hour. At Lady Bliss we call this "a glove made in heaven." Available through Entrenue at 800-368-7268.

Basic Vibrators

These babies have been around since the beginning of time! There is nothing fancy about them—they are smooth or shaped like a rounded erect penis and they just go buzz. You can get them in fun colors that can blink on and off. Usually, you control the speed at the base of the vibrator and use them for internal vaginal stimulation or to arouse the clitoris. You can actually use them to massage the shoulders and neck as well and then venture down to other interesting areas. At Lady Bliss parties, we suggest women use these on the inside of the shaft of their lovers' penis as a foreplay device, since most men love to have this area stimulated.

At Lady Bliss we carry Top Cat's Ultra Smooth Vibrator in our sex-toy party kits. It comes in a variety of pretty colors and does the trick perfectly. You can find this at www.americanlatex.com.

Topco Sales carries the Fiesta Vibes body massager. It comes in 7-inch, 6½-inch and 5-inch sizes. The packaging is rather tasteful as well. You can find this at www.topco-sales.com.

Cal Exotics carries a nice line of basic vibrators that they call Opulent-Lacquer Cote Massagers. The packaging for these products is attractive. They come in 4½-inch Compact Smooth, 4½-inch Opulent Compact Ridged, and Opulent 6-inch Ultra-Thin. You can find these at www.calexotics.com.

Bullets and Eggs

Bullets are fabulous, powerful and discreet clit stimulators. They get their name from the way they are shaped. Often larger bullets are called eggs. Little as they are, most bullets pack quite a vibrating punch. Many come with latex sleeves that can cover the bullet with different textures and contours. Some bullets are covered with a latex animal shape. Bullets are not meant to be used internally but are intended as the ultimate in clitoral stimulation. They come in many shapes, sizes and pretty colors. We love to joke and tell our customers that vibrating eggs are the perfect traffic busters. You can use them discreetly in the car to give yourself some good vibrations before facing the day!

One of our favorite bullets is the Bullet Blaster made by Golden Triangle. All we can say is, if you like your bullets to be super-charged, honey, this is the perfect toy for you. It comes with three sleeves that offer exhilarating contours for whatever mood you're in, as well as an attractive case for storing your bullet blaster after use. We have to give this toy two thumbs up! You can find it at www.holidayproducts.com.

Topco Sales makes a popular line of Petite Clit Exciters (micro bullets with pretty sleeves). You can use the wireless bullets alone or with the sleeves. They come with purple butterfly sleeves, yellow sunflower sleeves and pink starfish sleeves. You can find this at www.topco-sales.com

We also recommend Top Cat's Sparkling Egg multi-speed vibrator, which comes in a variety of attractive colors. You can find this at www.americanlatex.com.

The e-Vibe Vibrating Love Bullets from Topco Sales are worth considering as well. They come in a variety of attractive colors. You can find them at www.topco-sales.com.

Dual-Action Vibes

These toys have dual controls so you can change the amounts of clitoral and vaginal stimulation. The variations in these vibrators are usually in the quality of the materials, the number of speed settings, and whether or not the controller is attached or separate. Waterproof versions are available, but they are more limited in their functionality. These are usually the most expensive toys that your customers can buy, but they pack the best orgasmic punch for the money.

Our favorite dual-action vibrator is the Bunny Pearl by Top Cat. It has a pearl-filled shaft that vibrates while it rotates in different directions to pleasure the vagina while the head (the bunny's ears) gives the clit a twist of delight. We call it "The 30-second Orgasm" because this exquisite toy thrills you in multiple ways simultaneously. It gives many women a mind-blowing orgasm in…you guessed it…30 seconds! The reputation of the Bunny Pearl is reaching far and wide. It even appeared as a special guest star on HBO's "Sex and the City." You can find Lady Bliss's favorite Bunny Pearl at www.amer icanlatex.com.

"Extreme" toys offer extreme pleasure to your customers. Our top seller is the Extreme Erotic Pleasure Vibe. These babies are more powerful—and sometimes larger and more expensive—than their counterparts but well worth it. They offer the pearls of pleasure, as well as the most satisfying clit stimulators, along with cordless controls. You can find this at www.americanlatex.com.

Cal Exotics makes the Decadent Indulgence. This dual-action wireless vibrator comes with eight different levels of vibrating intensity, and three independent functions of shaft rotation, along with a powerful clitoral stimulator with its very own vibrator. You can find this at www.holidayproducts.com.

Realistic Vibrators

These toys look like the real thing, but with the added benefit of vibrating for extra stimulation. They both feel and look like a penis, down to realistic veins and testicles!

Top Cat makes the Silky Flesh Cock Vibe with Balls. It looks and feels like the real thing with the extra benefit of multi-speed vibration that will rock your world. You can find this at www.americanlatex.com.

White Caribbean realistic cordless vibes come in a variety of shapes and sizes, with powerful multi-speed vibration for extra realistic satisfaction. You can find these at www.holidayproducts.com.

The Vibro Realistic 6-inch and 8-inch multi-speed Vibrating Cock has the extra benefit of a suction cup, so you can stick it anywhere while enjoying realistic vibrating pleasure. You can find this at www.holidayproducts.com.

Mini Massagers

Small and discreet yet satisfying is the best way to describe a mini massager. Two little AA batteries are all it takes to power these babies but we can tell you, mini vibrating toys pack a punch like no other. There are many different mini massagers on the market: some look like lipstick cases, others literally fit in your pocket, and then there are those that fit on your finger (which are great to use on partners, too). Mini vibes are perfect for women on the run, or women who want small vibrators for discretion.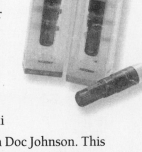

Probably one of the best known mini massagers is the I-Vibe Pocket Rocket from Doc Johnson. This little rocket is powerful enough to send you straight to the moon. You can find this at www.holidayproducts.com.

Topco Sales also makes a clever and discreet Vibrating Lipstick Secret Mini Massager that comes in fuchsia and pink. We think they work really well as either party gifts or hostess incentives.

There is no end to the adult toy makers' ingenuity! There is even a wireless vibrating "pen" that comes in a nice "pen case" with an extra battery. Working at the office will never be the same! You can find this at www.holidayproducts.com.

Another neat mini massager is Topco-Sales' Wild Mini Heart G Body Massager. The packaging is soft and feminine and the mini massager is made to hit your very sweet G-spot. You can also use it for clitoral stimulation. Available at www.topco-sales.com.

Waterproof Toys

Designed to be used in the bath, hot tub, shower or pool, these look like regular bath toys—including sponges, bunnies or birdies, and rubber duckies—but they vibrate in a way that gives rub-a-dub-dub a whole new meaning. *Note:* Always suggest that your customers use a silicone-based lube when playing with water toys. Water washes away natural body oils and fluids, and without enough slip and slide, water toys can cause irritation or pain instead of pleasurable sensations.

One of our top-selling waterproof toys is the Bathtub Birdie by Top Cat. Our motto is, it gives you a reason to sing in the shower. With its vibrating shaft and vibrating birdie beak that hits you just right, you can't go wrong. You can find this at www.americanlatex.com.

A really fun waterproof massager is the I Rub My Duckie Waterproof Personal Massager. It floats and vibrates too! You can find this at Entrenue at 800-368-7268.

Another top seller for Lady Bliss is the Junior Studded Waterproof Torpedo Vibe. You can use it in your favorite water environment or on dry land too. It has strong vibration with pleasure bumps all over to make your waterproof fun more enticing. Purchase at www.americanlatex.com.

G-Spot Vibrators

At Lady Bliss, we always encourage the women at our parties to figure out for themselves what turns them on. If they cannot tell their partners what they like in bed, how can they expect to be pleased? We hold the same opinion when it comes to women finding their G-spot, which many consider to be the promised land. Many women have described the G-spot orgasm as the most intense orgasm they have ever experienced. In fact, it is the source of and secret behind female ejaculation. Finding your G-spot expands your arousal options: you do not always need to be clitorally stimulated because the G-spot provides its own deep pleasure. In most women, the G-spot is located a few inches in, on the front of their pelvic wall. A partner can find it with by inserting a finger and making a "come here" gesture with it. For a small portion of women the G-spot is much farther back, and for another small portion, it is located closer to the vaginal opening. G-spot vibes have a slightly curved head to make it easy to find and stimulate this sacred spot. We always encourage the women at our parties to have their partners use it with them, so they will learn exactly where their "Glorious Spot" is located.

The differences between various G-spot vibrators are in the strength of their vibrations, the materials they are made of, the quality of the product, and whether they are waterproof.

A Lady Bliss favorite is the 8-inch Waterproof G-Spot from Top Cat. It not only hits your G-spot, but can also be used in the tub for wet and wild fun. It can be purchased at www.americanlatex.com.

Topco Sales makes the Celebrity Series Slimline G Vibes. The packaging is fairly tame with no nudity and is a perfect "first time" G-spot explorer vibe. We always encourage our customers to go on the hunt for this elusive spot with their partners, and these give them both an idea of where to find the promised land. You can find this at www.holidayproducts.com.

Another toy that is absolute heaven for G-spot stimulation is Top Cat's Erotic G-Spot Vibrator with Vibrating Egg attachment, which can be used for either anal or clitoral stimulation. However it's used, we call it the one-two erotic punch! You get twice the delight for the money. Look for this at www.americanlatex.com.

SALES TIPS: G-SPOT VIBES

Woman must appreciate and be interested in their G-spot to buy this product, so your goal is to get them interested in finding it. The G-spot has been associated with full-body orgasms, "gusher" orgasms and multiple orgasms. We have heard women explain that their clitoral orgasms are like a sneeze compared with the depth and power of their G-spot orgasms. That makes me want to find mine, how about you?

Finger Vibes

These are neat vibrating massagers that fit on one fingertip—or up to all ten. Some are even waterproof. These toys can be used as a general massager (or at least start out that way!) and for sensual play, hitting all of the erogenous zones of the body. Finger vibes are great toys for couples as they can be used dynamically in different  sexual positions—to stimulate the clitoris or nipples, to stroke the penis or scrotum and whatever else comes naturally.

One of our faves is the Busy Beaver from Top Cat. It comes complete with powerful multi-speed vibration and fits on your finger with a wrist strap to give yourself precise pleasure. We always suggest to our customers that they share the love and use it with a partner too. You can find this at www. holidayproducts.com.

The Dolfinger from Benwa also fits on your finger and has a 6-speed dual-action vibration mode controller. Another neat feature is that you can take the bullet vibrator in and out of the Dolfinger so you can use the bullet separately if you wish. You can find this at www.benwa.com.

Fukuoku makes well-known finger massagers and finger vibes, including the 9000 Finger Tip Massager and the Wrist Held Three Finger Tip Massager. These toys make your fingers into erotic body massagers that can be used on all of your erogenous zones. You can purchase them through Entrenue at 800-368-7268.

Undercover Undies

Not only are these vibrating panties cute, fashionable and discreet, but they pack a punch too! Undercover undies are specially designed to get your groove on in public. A hidden pocket in the front crotch area holds the egg or bullet vibrator of your choice (and many undies also come with one). All you have to do is set the vibrations and let the pleasure shine through. Some models come with remote control, so you can hand over the driving to your partner. You can replace the vibe at will, so one time you might want to use a cordless vibe, and another time, one with a cord.

Cal Exotics makes Wild Exotics Remote Control Vibrating Panties. Made of 100 percent cotton, Wild Exotic Panties are Brazilian-cut thongs that are not only made to get your groove on, but are also comfortable and washable. They come with a powerful ZR-5000 stimulator that fits in a special spot in the panties. One size fits most. You can find these at www.calexotics.com.

Another great Cal Exotics product is the Remote Control Vibrating Panty. This vibrating panty combines comfort with a remote boasting a range of 15 to 20 feet. Just think of the possibilities! During foreplay you can let your lover turn you on at will. Now that's a vibrating experience! Available at www.calexotics.com.

Cal Exotics also has the Wild Exotic Waterproof Vibrating Panty that you can use while playing adult water sports. They can be purchased at www.calexotics.com.

Hands-Free Pleasure Vibes

These vibrators usually come with an elastic strap that you adjust around your pelvis, legs or waist, placing the vibrator right over the clitoris. These toys allow you to lie back, relax and adjust the controls to the level of stimulation you desire. They come in many designs, with the vibes often nestled in a heart or butterfly-shaped pocket that can be positioned to hit your sweet spot just right. These vibrators are great to use during intercourse for extra clitoral attention. Hands-free vibes also come with G-spot and vaginal arousal attachments.

Tera Patrick's Pulsating Heart Vibe sells quite well at home parties, and is a very nice product—but beware, the packaging shows Tera Patrick demonstrating the product. Though her top is covered everything else is displayed. Nudity on these types of products seems to be the norm, as the manufactures want to show you how the products work. You can find this at www.holidayproducts.com.

Another popular hands-free pleasure vibe is Cal Exotics' Remote Control Butterfly. It has comfortable adjustable straps that fit snugly around your hips to help the butterfly hit you just right and is controlled by a small and compact control that can turn you off and on! Beware of nudity on the packaging. Available at www.holidayproducts.com.

Doc Johnson's Strap On, Hands Free Butterfly Multi-Speed Pleasure Vibe has a dildo connected to the vibrator, so not only will it hit your sweet spot in all the right places, but it fills you up with pleasure too. The straps fit snugly and comfortably around your hips. The packaging on this product is nice; there's no nudity and it's very feminine. You can find this at www.holidayproducts.com.

Contour Vibrators

These vibes are feminine in appearance and are made for women with a sensitive clitoris, as they provide gentle stimulation. They are smooth and made of plastic or jelly. One of our favorite lines is the Candida Royalle Contour Vibe collection. Ms. Royalle, once a famous porn star and now a producer, understands the sensual needs of women and her toys truly reflect that. Candida Royalle has many different contour vibrators in her special collection dedicated to fit women's special needs:

Candida Royalle's family of Natural Contour Massagers include the 4-inch Petite, 4 3/4-inch Medium and the 7½-inch Large. All of these massagers are of the highest quality, with a 3-speed slide switch and discreet low noise level. To purchase, call Entrenue at 800-368-7268.

She just added to her family of successful contour massagers by adding the Jolie Waterproof Contour Vibrator. Tiny and discreet, it packs a powerful vibration in its feminine, sturdy and pretty frame. You can purchase this from Entrenue at 800-368-7268.

Royalle even has her own G-spot contour called the Ultime. The 4½ x 1-inch insertable end curves upward towards that very special spot, while the handle reaches up to hit the clitoris for a double whammy of pleasure. Available through Entrenue at 800-368-7268.

ELEVEN

Couples Toys

Not surprisingly, couples toys are very popular at Lady Bliss home parties. Because they are made for two instead of just one, they help partners find new fun in pleasing each other during lovemaking. The most common couples toys combine a cock ring or penis sleeve for the man and some kind of stimulator, usually a vibrator, for the woman. Sometimes the vibrator is built into the cock ring or sleeve, or is removable while he's still wearing it, so it can be used creatively in sexual positions that require some extra zing. Some cock rings just have a "clitoral bump" rather than a vibrator built into the ring.

Cock rings are worn at the base of the penis, to help a man maintain a harder erection for longer period of time. Because the ring wraps around him tightly, it keeps the blood flow in the penis, which not only makes him harder longer but provides him with a much more enjoyable orgasm.

Penis sleeves can cover the entire penis or just a portion of it. They essentially provide the same benefits that a cock ring does but offer slightly different sensations. They are perfect for nights when you "have a headache" and aren't up for a hand job.

Cock Rings with Clitoral Stimulators

These simple toys are perfect for first-time toy users. Couples with no prior vibrator experience often find them much less intimidating than a full-fledged vibe. We carry one that looks almost like a soap dish, with a ring for the penis, pleasure nubs that feel good on the skin, and a little bump that can hit the clitoris whether the woman is on top or in the missionary position.

Like all of the other toys we have described, there are many different types and a variety of manufacturers who make these kinds of products. But one that we carry, which does very well, is Holiday Products' Deluxe Royal Stimulator. It has a hole in the middle to hug his penis tightly yet comfortably, and a little clit stimulator for her. On the body of the ring are pleasure bumps

SALES TIPS: COUPLES TOYS

The best way to sell cock rings and penis sleeves is to demonstrate on one of the dildos that you sell. If you don't carry a dildo, buy one for this purpose. It is important for women to see how these fit on their man and to understand fully how they work. If you do this, your sales will increase greatly. Cock rings and similar toys are also your chance to up-sell lubes. Since many couples toys work best when lubed up, encourage your customers to buy a lube or two that will work well with these his-and-hers toys.

for added stimulation. You can find this at www.hol-idayproducts.com.

Top Cat also has an excellent soft and stretchy silicone Cock Ring with Clit Bumper. This ring has stimulating bumps on the clit bumper and along the ring for him to add extra stimulation. To purchase, go to www.americanlatex.com.

Cal Exotics carries the Senso Lover with a clit bumper and stimulation bumps for extra sensation. You can find this at www.calexotics.com.

Vibrating Cock Rings

These are the ultimate couples toy, as they pleasure both parties. They turn his penis into a vibrator for all-out pleasure-packed fun. You can buy these with large, non-removable egg-like vibrators and stimulation nubs all over the ring, or with a little bullet vibrator that can be removed. Some rings even come with two vibes for double the pleasure—his and hers. Some of these toys have vibration controls.

One of our very favorite couples toys is the Clearly Sensual Cock Ring. This thing will rock your world. The silicone cock ring stretches so it will fit snugly on the shaft of his penis, while the powerful bullet gives you a clitoral treat. The bullet can even be removed so you can use it when doing the dirty in other positions. We give this toy two thumbs up. You can find this at www.holidayproducts.com.

Another favorite is the Jelly Vibrating Wittle Wabbit Ring. It has a ring for him that helps him stay harder longer, while making his orgasms much more enjoyable, and vibrating ears to hit your sweet clitoral spot, and a little tail that just tickles the anus to add extra stimulation. This little rascal can be found at www.holi dayproducts.com.

Cal Exotics' Ring of Passion has a nice cock ring for him and a vibe with extra stimulation bumps for her. It can be purchased at www.holidayproducts.com.

SALES TIPS: VIBRATING COCK RINGS

Since these are easy sells, give partygoers use-oriented advice: Always use lubricant with these toys. If you pull his little hairs while putting it on, he's not going to play with you any more, plus he'll love the feeling of you stroking him with lube before attaching the toy. If the woman orgasms first, turn the vibrator around to hit him in that very sensitive area between the balls and the shaft of the penis. It will give him an orgasm that is out of this world—he will love you forever!

Penis Sleeves with Vibrators

These toys fit completely over the whole penis with the head sticking out, or over a portion of the penis so he can feel the inside of the vagina. They have a vibrator that fits on top (which can usually be removed), and may or may not have an extra attachment that goes around the testicles to provide extra stimulation for him. Because these sleeves "hug" the penis they don't need an anchor. Most men love to have their balls massaged with a vibrator, and this toy is a hands-free way to achieve that. (*Note*: Since these are a snug fit, you need lots of lube to get them on comfortably.)

Topco Sales offers the Smooth Moves Cock Cage with Wireless Vibrator for her. It fits over half of the penis so he still has plenty of feeling. This toy also features "excitement beads" that add extra stimulation for him and her. You can find this at www.topco-sales.com.

We also like Topco's Smooth Moves Vibrating Silicone Masturbator with added Wireless Vibration for her. This "cage" covers the whole penis, allowing just the head to stick out. You'll find the extra benefit of "excitement beads" in this one as well. Available at www.topco-sales.com.

Another great product is the silicone Invisible Man. It's a complete penile support system that has the added benefit of wireless vibration for her. It has deep ridges for extra stimulation and can be adjusted to accommodate length. It also comes with a testicle strap that will make his orgasms that much more enjoyable and keep him coming back for more. To purchase go to www.topco-sales.com.

Masturbation Sleeves

Designed for male masturbation, these toys hug the penis tightly and may or may not have pleasure beads inside the sleeve. When used properly with lots of lubricant, they slide up and down his shaft until he experiences the ultimate of pleasure. He can use this by himself or you can use it as a "tonight

I have a headache" aid. Saves your wrist and makes him smile!

At Lady Bliss we carry Benwa's Veronica Pleasure Sleeve in our home-party kits and it does very well. We not only describe it as a "honey I have a headache" toy, but one that can bring some variety into your foreplay action, getting him nice and hard and ready to go. It also makes a great "fun" gift for him. You can find this at www.benwa.com.

Top Cat's pleasure sleeve is called Pleasure Buddy and has pearls of ecstasy inside the shaft so he gets extra stimulation. You can purchase this at www.americanlatex.com.

Top Cat also carries the Fun Pal. It has no pleasure pearls inside but looks like a vagina that's soft and nice and snug inside. To purchase, go to www.americanlatex.com.

> **SALES TIPS: MASTURBATION SLEEVES**
>
> Suggest to your female customers that they need to purchase something just for their man so that he doesn't feel left out, especially if they are purchasing items solely for their own pleasure.

Nipple Toys

These unique gadgets are worth mentioning because some women (and men!) love to have their nipples played with during lovemaking. And what better way to do that than with a toy made just for that purpose? Nipple stimulators are little clamps or pumps that fit on the nipples. Some clamps come with an attached vibrator for extra stimulation. Nipple pumps provide both gentle suction and pressure.

Cal Exotics has the Sensual Titillation Nipple Suckers that can be used by him or her. They gently hug and tease the nipples with soft suction. You can find these at www.holidayproducts.com.

There is quite a variety of nipple clamps to choose from. One that looks more feminine and not as fetishistic is the Mini Clamps with Violet Beads. The packaging is tasteful as well. These can be found at www.holidayproducts.com.

Cal Exotics has their Waterproof Wireless Nipple Arousers under their Wicked line. They are feminine-looking and can be used for adult water play or on dry land. But beware, there are bare breasts on the packaging. You can find these at www.calexotics.com.

TWELVE

Anal Toys

A nal toys are used to either massage or penetrate the anus. There is a surprising array of toys to choose from—including large ones, small ones, ones that vibrate, ones with a suction cup, etc. There is something for everyone, whether curious first-timer or experienced player. Anal play is a sensitive subject, we know, but let's face it, it can be very pleasurable for relaxed and willing people who have a back-door ready for pleasing.

Unlike the vagina, the anus does not have natural lubrication, so we always say, "Use lube, more lube, tons of lube!" The wetter it is, the better it's going to feel. So when you display and sell anal toys, make sure to partner them with a variety of lubricants—water-based, silicone-based and oil-based.

Cleanliness is one of the most important aspects of anal play. Remind customers never to use a toy for anal play and then insert it into the vagina without first cleaning it thoroughly with anti-bacterial soap or toy cleaner. The natural bacteria in the anus can cause serious infections in the vagina.

SALES TIPS: ANAL TOYS

Explaining anal play is always going to be a challenge because this part of our anatomy is considered taboo and against biblical principles to some. But we all know people do it, they just don't want to admit it. The best way to approach this subject is just to be frank about it. People are curious so you need to ex-plain that if done right it feels good. We suggest that if people have questions and are interested in exploring safe, clean anal play they should watch Nina Hartley's video "Guide to Anal Sex." She talks about this very delicate area in depth and provides all the info you need to know to enjoy "back door love."

At Lady Bliss parties we wait until we've talked about all the other toys, then gently introduce anal toys with the Tantus Silicone anal plug. We explain that this is the "last frontier" but if done right, with lots of lube and a good bullet vibrator to stimulate your sweet spot, it will give you a kind of pleasure you have never experienced before. Like they say on "Sex and the City," God gave you that hole too, so why not use it!

On a side note, men like to use anal toys as well, which can add an exciting new twist when you play together underneath the sheets. Just because a man enjoys anal stimulation does not mean he will develop a sexual preference for men; it just means he enjoys the added stimulation. The man's prostate, which is a man's equivalent of the G-spot, can only be accessed through the anus, with a toy or a finger. Just like our G-spot brings us joy, the prostate brings men much pleasure when played with during lovemaking.

A terrific product for exploring anal play is Anal Ease. It has special ingredients to give the outside of the anus a

nice tingly, numb feel so insertion is much more comfortable. But don't use this as an excuse not to get the anus nice and ready. It needs to be "played with" just like all of your other erogenous zones so it's ready for love too. You can find this at www.holidayproducts.com.

Butt Plugs

These toys are designed to be inserted, and then left in place for a while. They are not intended to be thrust in and out. These toys give the rectum a feeling of fullness, while other erogenous zones are being played with. These are perfect toys to help train and relax the anal muscles. Butt plugs come in many sizes but all have a similar shape: narrow on the top for easy insertion, thicker through the base, and then narrow toward the bottom. All have a flared base to keep them in place, so they do not get lost in the rectum. Butt plugs come in both vibrating and non-vibrating models.

Top Cat has the vibrating and non-vibrating Jelly Butt Plug that is much thinner at the top and gets thicker in the middle. It also has a base that can be used in a harness for those who like to live on the wilder side of life. They come in a variety of pretty colors as well. You can find these at www.americanlatex.com.

Another interesting butt plug is called the Little Zinger. It's smaller and more comfortable for those who are new to anal exploration. It comes in pretty colors too. These can be purchased at www.holidayproducts.com.

Doc Johnson has the vibrating I-Plug with a 5-speed dual action anal pleasure mode controller. It has a thin base for comfort with a pleasure bump in the middle. The packaging for this product is nice as well. You can find this at www.holi dayproducts.com.

Corkscrews

Looking just like their name, these have ridges up and down their shaft so that you can give yourself or your partner the pleasurable sensation of "screwing" by twisting the toy in and out. Like butt plugs, these have a narrow head, a thicker middle and a base for safety. They come in both vibrating and non-vibrating models.

Top Cat carries the 6-inch Corkscrew with a suction cup for easy use either by yourself or with a partner. It comes in a non-vibrating and vibrating model. It has a smaller tip for easy insertion, then gets thicker in the middle. You can find this at www.americanlatex.com.

Top Cat also carries the 6-inch Neo-Gel Twist that is non-vibrating for twisting anal pleasure. Please note, these products can also be used vaginally. But make sure that you empha-size to your customers that they use separate toys for anal and vaginal use. These are available at www.americanlatex.com.

Topco Sales has the Lil Piggy Butt Plug, which is a per-fect starter toy for new anal pleasure seekers. Though it is called a plug, it does have a corkscrew-type body, which pro-vides a smooth comfortable fit, with a handle that can be used to screw in and out. Beware, this packaging does have nudity, showing a woman's backside. You can find this at www.topco-sales.com.

Anal Beads

These come on a nylon string in a variety of sizes from little to quite large, for all comfort levels. Anal beads are smooth

balls made of jelly, rubber, silicone or plastic. We always advise that you buy a jelly or softer anal bead, since plastic beads can sometimes have rough edges as a result of their manufacturing and the skin in the anus can tear easily. Once the beads are inserted, you or your partner should take them out slowly during orgasm for a pleasurable one-two punch.

Benwa's soft jelly anal beads have soft edges so they won't hurt during insertion or removal. They come in small, medium and large. If you sell these in your kit, make sure that your customers know to use lots of lube! You can find these at www.benwa.com.

Acrylic Glitter Stixx Anal Wand is essentially anal beads on a stick. What's nice about these is that they are acrylic and non-porous so they can be cleaned easily and effectively. Because they are on a stick they are easily insertable either by the user or the partner. You can find these at www.holiday products.com.

Vibrating Anal Beads give you the same sensation that anal beads do, with an extra kick. Instead of a string at the end they have a larger bead that can be used as a handle to pull them in and out, and start from small to large for extra stimulation, while having multiple speeds to give your backside some good vibrations. Again, these work well on your own or with a partner. You can find these at www.holidayproducts.com.

Cleanliness Is Next to Godliness

Toy care is an important part of toy fun. If you are going to stick something inside your body, you must keep it very clean so you that you or your partner do not get an infec-

tion. At Lady Bliss home parties we push this concept over and over again because we want our customers to have a safe and pleasurable experience with their toys. That means before even engaging in sextoy fun make sure your hands are clean, and before using any toy give it one more wipe down with an antibacterial soap (be careful when cleaning toys with batteries) or a special cleaner made specifically for sex toys. There are many toy cleaners now on the market, including individually wrapped wipes. It should go without saying that after you use a toy, clean it thoroughly with soap and hot water to make sure all bodily juices have been removed.

Store sex toys in a clean, cool, dry place. Before putting them away, make sure they are completely dry, since water and dampness can break down the material of some sex toys and ruin them.

Additionally, before you use any of your toys make sure to inspect them carefully for cracks that can harbor bacteria or cause the toy to scratch or break off inside you. Sex toys are not made to last forever, so you need to retire well-worn toys when they look like they have had enough fun for their lifetime.

There are some great products out there that help with toy care. One that sells well for Lady Bliss is called Mighty Tidy Toy Cleaner, which you can purchase through Entrenue 800-368-7268, or Before & After, which you can purchase from www.holidayproducts.com. Whatever brand you buy, the most important thing you can do is educate your customers about toy care, because quite frankly, they may have no clue. At Lady Bliss we always advise our customers to clean not only with toy cleaner, but also with antibacterial soap (very carefully with vibrators, so you don't get water into any of the working parts) just to make doubly sure all is well cleansed.

THIRTEEN

Lubricants

Lubricants are a must-have when playing with sex toys. The purpose of sex toys is to create F-U-N, but if you try to stick a toy in a place that is not ready for it, especially the vagina, it is anything *but* fun. That's why lube was created. Spread the word: "The wetter the better!"

Not all women want to use lubricants all the time, but most woman require lubricants at least some of the time. Some women don't slick up as easily early in their menstrual cycle. Others are drier when they use the Pill. Lube makes these times much more fun. Lube is also a must for women as they get older and closer to menopause. As we age, our vaginas naturally produce fewer juices. Liberal use of a lubricant, both during sex and when using dildos or other sex toys, makes penetration easier, more comfortable and much more fun. Younger women, even if they are naturally juicy, often find that lubes can increase or prolong their sensations. And don't forget that using lubes encourages foreplay, since someone's got to apply it!

Water-based Lubes

We prefer water-based lubricants, as they are less likely to cause irritation and yeast infections in those women who are highly sensitive. They also wash off easily and won't stain your sheets, toys or clothes. Lastly and very importantly, water-based lubes are condom compatible. You can buy plain or flavored water-based lubes, as there are many different varieties.

One of our favorite lubes is called Liquid Silk. Made by a little-known company from the United Kingdom, it's one of the best lubes on the market today. This stuff really feels like silk on your skin, is completely safe for women who are prone to yeast infections, is completely water based with no glycerin, and does not get gummy and sticky. Men love how it feels, too! You can buy it through Entrenue, at 800-368-7268. (You can also buy sampler packs, which make great gifts for those who buy toys.)

Another fabulous water-based lube is Astroglide. It sells very well at LadyBliss.com. It is long-lasting and top quality. You can purchase this prod-

SALES TIPS: LUBRICANTS

Let customers try the products by passing them around and rubbing a drop or two in their hands. It is a good idea to carry small samples of the lubes that you carry with you. You can give these out to customers who place big orders, or customers who purchase sex toys that need lube. This will make your guests more likely to try them and later buy them from you.

A NOTE ON LUBES

Always make your customers aware that women who are prone to yeast infections should avoid any lubricant with glycerin or sugar (which many flavored lubricants contain) or the spermicide Nonoxynol-9. These ingredients can promote the growth of yeast cultures in women who are sensitive to them. At Lady Bliss we make it a practice to know what each product we carry is made of, so that we're able not only to tell our customers of the products' benefits but also to warn them of things to watch out for.

Couples using condoms or dental dams should be careful to avoid using any kind of oil-based lubricant. This includes body oil, baby oil, massage oil, and some pleasure-inducing creams for him and her. Oil will deteriorate latex and can cause condoms or dental dams to break.

uct through B Cummings at 800-226-6464. (You can also buy sampler packs for gifts.)

Sensual Power is a non-sticky, non-glycerin, non-irritating moisturizing lubricant that is the next generation of personal lubricant technology. You can find this through Entrenue at 800-368-7268.

Silicone Lubes

These lubes are very slippery and tend not to gum up the way some water-based lubricants do. They also tend to last longer (depending on how good the brand is), so they are perfect for extended play sessions. Silicone lubricants are also ideal for use in the water and for anal sex. Unlike water-based lubes, silicone lubes don't wash off easily (unless you are using soap). Silicone is safe to use with latex and condoms as

it does not break down the material. But silicone lube *can* ruin silicone sex toys—so it is best to use a condom on your toys if you're going to use a silicone-based lubricant.

One of our favorite silicone lubes is Pjur Eros Body Glide Silicone Lubricant. It's a little more expensive than some of the others but worth it. It's great stuff. You can buy this through B. Cummings Company at 800-226-6464.

Another wonderful silicone lube is called Wet Platinum. The name says it all: this product feels wetter than wet. You can also buy this through B Cummings at 800-226-6464.

I-lube from Doc Johnson is a trusted name in lubes. You can find it at www.holidayproducts.com.

FOURTEEN

Romance Products

Romance products help couples reconnect and explore different ways to fire up the heat between the sheets. Additionally, romance products tend be a little softer (or at least appear that way), and so do very well with customers who may be a little shy when it comes to erotic products. Of course, there are also romance products that cater to couples who like things on the wild side.

Romance products come in many shapes and sizes. In this section you will learn about all the exciting and delicious ways that you can add a little romance into your customers' (or your own) love lives.

Massage Kits, Books and Videos

Massage is often referred to as the touch of love. There is nothing more enjoyable than spending the evening with the one you adore, giving or receiving a sensual massage. It's a wonderful intimacy-building tool for relationships and a fun form of foreplay. The majority of sex-toy party companies carry massage products, which are always top sellers. There are many resources available that will give your customers great ideas on how to add massage into their lovemaking.

The Hot Massage Kit from Lover's Choice is one of our favorite massage toys. When you take the heart-shaped toy out of the beautiful packaging, you'll see that it contains a clear pink liquid, with a little tab that activates the heart to heat up. It stays hot for up to 45 minutes and feels absolutely fabulous sliding up and down your body. You can use it over and over again: just boil it in water until all of the crystals are gone, cool it to room temperature, and voilà—it's ready for the next session! You can find this at www.loverschoice.com.

If you love back massages you will find everything you need in the Massage Kit and Game by Enrichments, which makes romantic products for lovers. It comes with edible warming oil, massage oil and lotion along with a spinner board and cards to enhance the touch of love. Enrichments does not sell directly to the public. Contact Entrenue at 800-368-7268 if you would like more information on these products.

An absolutely marvelous massage book and video set is Erotic Massage: The Touch of Love. It gives step-by-step instructions on how to give your lover the gift of touch. You can find this through Entrenue at 800-368-7268.

Massage Oils and Lotions

These are a must-have for your kit, not only for the customers who may not be into sex toys, but for those who  want to boost the romance in their lives. The vast array of massage oils and lotions guarantees something for everyone. There are oils that glow in the dark, tasty edible creams, lotions for a light touch and smell, and aromatherapy oils with a thicker feel and more potent smell. There are even very light massage oils with added pheromones to get your groove on!

Classic Erotica's Loving Touch Aphrodisiac Massage Oil comes in nice packaging with even nicer fragrances. You can also buy it in sample size, which makes a nice gift or giveaway at your parties. You can find this at www.holidayproducts.com.

Once of our top-selling massage oils is Cal Exotics' Citrus Basil Massage Oil with Pheromones. It's also available as a lotion. It's light, it has a refreshing scent and both men and women love it. Just think, while you're giving a massage you're also stirring up his sexual urges! You can find this at www.holidayproducts.com.

If you're looking for a massage lotion, Classic Erotica's Erotica

SALES TIPS: MASSAGE OILS AND LOTIONS
Sell the health and intimacy-building benefits of massage. Let customers touch, smell and taste the flavored products. Rub massagers along their backs, or encourage them to do the same.

Creamy Oil sells well for Lady Bliss. It comes in a variety of enticing scents and appeals to those who don't like the feel of oil on their skin. You can buy this through www.holiday products.com.

Couples Games

These romantic games help couples reconnect and build stronger communication skills. Most American women will tell you that their partners are not very romantic. Unfortu-

nately, men sometimes need to be trained and shown the tricks of the trade. Some games are sex-oriented, while others are more "romantic." Inexpensive dice games are simple and loads of fun to play, helping to make lovemaking more adventurous. There are card and board games to enhance oral sex, to teach the Kama Sutra and to build better foreplay skills. There are scratch-off cards that incorporate a sexy element of surprise and romance, and there are bathing games that encourage sensual fun while taking a bath together. You should choose games for your kit that you believe will best suit the needs and interests of your customers.

One of our favorite games is Passion Throw, an erotic dice game. Rather than using a board, you roll the dice on a blanket, which you can spread out by the fireplace, take on a picnic, or lounge on at the beach. You take turns, roll the dice, lie down on the blanket and go to town! You can purchase this product through Entrenue at 800-368-7268.

52 Weeks of Naughty Nights is an inexpensive scratch-off card game made by one of our favorite companies, Lover's Choice. There are cards for him and her. Taking turns, you scratch off a card and surprise each other with the naughty encounter. It makes a great gift for the one you love. You can find this at www.loverschoice.com.

Another fun game is the Dirty Week-ender Kit by Lover's Choice. It comes in a cute box with a spinner card, twelve surprise cards, four tealights, sizzling body candy (guess where you put that?), sensual bondage tie, flavored massage oil and pleasure balm. Available at www.loverschoice.com.

Romance Kits

These are a perfect way to say "I love you." You can buy kits that come with rose petals, edible massage oils, bubble bath, body massagers and more. There are specialty kits with light bondage gear for an erotic evening of tie-me-up, as well as kits with champagne

SALES TIPS: KITS AND GAMES

Don't show partygoers a closed box with a game inside and expect them to buy it. Games will sell better if you open them up, explain them and pass them around. Romantic gifts sell best if you encourage customers to imagine how these products could introduce an evening of romance.

flutes, tasty treats and candles. These are great products to include in your kit because they make ideal bridal, anniversary and Valentine's Day gifts.

If you want to offer your customers a top-of-the-line romance kit we recommend the Deluxe Bed of Roses made

by Lover's Choice. A black silk bag contains the ingredients for a night of five-star romance: over 200 rose-scented silk petals, edible chocolate-flavored massage oil, rose-scented bubble bath, an old fashioned-massager, four tea lights, a card inviting your lover to indulge, and Bliss Balm clitoral cream. Talk about giving your lover the night of a lifetime! It's romance at its finest. You can find this and many other romance products at www.loverschoice.com.

Topco Sales has come out with a fully-packed romance kit called A Thousand and One Nights Romance collection. It comes with massage oil, warming edible massage oils and other edible delights. Also included is a feather tickler, a romantic candle, a wooden body massager, incense and a lovers scroll. This can be purchased at www.holidayproducts.com.

Another great kit is the Sinclair Intimacy Institute's 52 Weeks of Passionate Sex. Their kit is similar to the Lover's Choice kit, but more on the naughty side. It comes with a "personal massager" (a vibrator), a book of erotica, a candle, a Do Not Disturb sign, scented rose petals, 24 love cards, a feather tickler for teasing and a blindfold. You can find this at www.intimacyinstitute.com.

FIFTEEN

Tasty Treats

Sensual and scrumptious sexual enhancers are carried by every party company in various forms. These products are used during oral sex for greater or tastier sensations, or for straight sexual pleasure. Some of these products make orgasms much more intense with the use of menthol or assist in oral sex by numbing your tongue. One thing you can count on, they are guaranteed to give your libido a boost and enhance your sexual experience.

Warming Oils and Lotions

Available in an assortment of delicious flavors such as champagne, ambrosia, and white peach, these are a yummy way to turn your lover into a midnight snack. These sweet temptations glide on any and all erogenous zones of the body. Just think about how good it would feel to have your lover put something warm and sticky on your nipples, and then lick it off. These tasty treats work best when you rub, blow and lick the skin where they're applied because they get nice and toasty that way. These oral treats can be thick and sticky or light with an oilier base, perfect for massage. Please note that many of these products contain glycerin and sugar, which can cause yeast infections in women who are prone to them.

One of our favorite warming oils is Satori Oil of Love in White Peach. It tastes like a peach martini, all the while making your lover's parts warm and delicious. It doesn't heat up as much as other products on the market, which is great for people who are more sensitive, and it is not too heavy and sticky, as some lotions can be. This "oil of love" is truly lovely! It comes in beautiful packaging, and is a good bargain. You can buy this through Entrenue at 800-368-7268.

Hot Licks is probably the best warming lotion on the market today. It comes in tasty flavors and gets very warm when you rub, blow and lick. This product is a perfect one for hot sweet loving. You can find this product at www.holi dayproducts.com.

Love Licker Warming Lotion is absolutely delicious, and packaged in adorable little liquor bottles! It comes in flavors like Virgin Strawberry, Sex on the Beach and Malibu Screw. These make great gifts and will bring lots of giggles at your parties. They are available through Entrenue at 800-368-7268.

Flavored Lubes

These lubes are made strictly for oral sex. They do not get hot or do anything other than flavor your lover's privates

with such delicious flavors as chocolate mint, juicy fruit, lemon drop and wild cherry. Flavored lubricants add such a sweet ingredient to regular oral sex that all the party companies carry tasty lubes in one flavor or another.

If you like the taste of Wrigley's Juicy Fruit gum, then you'll love ForPlay's Juicy Fruit tasty lube! It comes in attractive packaging, and unlike some other flavored lubes, it is water based and condom compatible. To purchase, call B. Cummings Company at 800-226-6464.

A great-tasting flavored lube that is also a great buy is Top Cat's Rain. Our favorite is strawberry, but it comes in a variety of flavors. You can purchase it at www.americanlatex.com.

"Wet" is a popular brand for flavored lubes. The only downside is that it's available at most drug stores so your customers may have it already. However, it is a brand name that people who have some knowledge of erotic products recognize as an excellent product. You can buy neat little pillow packs perfect for hostess gifts. To purchase, call B Cummings Company at 800-226-6464.

Tasty Powders

These candied powders can be sprinkled like fairy dust. They feel like real powder to the touch, but taste like sweet nothing! Most come with a feather duster to tickle and tease your lover's body. Popular flavors include strawberry, cherry and honey.

Products by Kama Sutra are always a favorite among partygoers. They make a wonderful honey dust, and now have raspberry kiss and tangerines & crème flavors. Yum! You can find these at www.kamasutra.com.

One of our favorite candied body powders is Topco Sales' Tasty Tickles in Wild Strawberry, which does well at Lady Bliss Home Parties. It comes in a cute little tin with a spoon and feather duster to help entice your lover. You can find this at www.holidayproducts.com.

Tickle'n Taste Tasty Edible Dust is also a favorite among party guests. Available in a variety of yummy flavors, it comes with an attractive little duster. To purchase, go to www.holidayproducts.com

SALES TIPS: TASTY TREATS

The only way to sell tasty lubes and lotions is to let women taste them, and the best way to sell body products is to have women try them. So don't hesitate to pass these around the party. Remind customers that the only limitation to indulging in these treats is their imagination. These sexy treats are low in calories and high in satisfaction. They'll burn off any extra calories with good sweet loving.

Body Chocolates

These treats transform your lover into a human chocolate sundae. They are usually made of gourmet chocolate, in flavors such as raspberry chocolate, milk chocolate, chocolate mint and white chocolate. These decadent delights can be messy, so you want to plan ahead and spread out a sheet or towel for easy cleanup later.

Two of our favorites at Lady Bliss are Naked and Naughty Chocolate Finger

Paints (doesn't this help evoke some delicious thoughts?), available in chocolate and white chocolate, and Lickit & Luvitt Chocolate Love Cream, with almond, chocolate extreme, mocha, raspberry, chocolate supreme and white chocolate flavors. Both are well-made gourmet chocolate and make for some great chocolate loving. You can find these at Entrenue at 800-368-7268.

Body Butters and Frostings

These tasty delights for cooking outside the kitchen are usually thick and creamy, perfect for smearing on and licking off. They come in luscious flavors like lemon chiffon, cherry, and kiwi pie. We say, if you can make him taste like a kiwi pie, going down is worth the trip.

Ceduxion Body Butter is one of the best on the market in our opinion, and it comes in a variety of yummy flavors. The Key Lime is to die for; like we always say, who wouldn't want to snack on a penis that tastes like Key Lime pie? To make things even sweeter, the folks who run the place are great. You can find them at www.1on1bodycare.com

Chocoholic Body Frosting is by far the best-tasting chocolate made for loving. These folks actually make G-rated gourmet chocolates on top of their erotic line, and we have to say they're divine. You can find them at www.gourmetchocolate.com

Lickable Sprays and Whipped Creams

These tasty treats can be sprayed or smoothed on anywhere and licked off with tantalizing tongue action, a sweet and sexy way to explore each other's bodies. They are made for tasty pleasure, pure and simple.

A lickable spray that does well for Lady Bliss is called Delicious Kisses. It comes in a variety of yummy flavors. Just

think of the fun your party guests will have when they spray and lick! You can find this at Entrenue at 800-368-7268.

One of the most popular whipped body creams is Whipped Crème by Topco Sales. They even have Whipped Crème with Candy Sprinkles as well as a variety of other flavors. These are a lot of fun to use on the one you love when you're in the mood for hot sticky sex. You can find this product at www.holidayproducts.com.

SIXTEEN

Bath & Body Products

Sometimes feeling sexy has nothing to do with having sex. How you feel in your skin is just as important. Carrying some appealing bath products in your party kit will expand your sensual offerings for your customers—especially those who may not be interested in the toys, lubes and so forth. Taking baths together is a romantic, relaxing way for couples to reconnect, whether as the first step in an erotic evening or the culmination of the evening itself. It's also a fun way for single women to indulge themselves, or get in the mood for a hot date. There are so many different bath products on the market—bubbles that glow in the dark, aromatherapy oils to wash your cares away, bath salts to draw impurities from your body—that we can't begin to detail them all.

The majority of sex-toy party companies carry a line of private-label body products, but all of these lines have similar offerings: body washes and sprays, lotions and moisturizers, and pheromone colognes.

After-Bath Spray and Bath Gels

Bath gels and sprays sell well at home parties because they are not very expensive and often have special ingredients, such as pheromones, that enhance the libido. Not only do they have pleasing scents, but they can really perk up your morning shower!

Kama Sutra's Treasure of the Sea comes in a beautiful tin with a loofah sponge and a seashell scoop for the bath salts. Swirl it in as you run the tub to release the intoxicating scent, and then watch as it turns your bath a beautiful shade of blue. We have had women buy this product five at a time to give as gifts for their girlfriends. You can find this at www.kama-sutra.com

Lover's Choice makes bubble bath in a variety of romantic scents that you can find in their romance kits, as well as on their own. You can find these at www.lovers choice.com.

A really fun bubble bath to offer in your kit is Sexy Suds Glow in the Dark Bubble Bath. This product does well at Lady Bliss home parties. You just put it in the light for about a minute or so, pour it in the tub, turn off the lights, jump in and watch all your favorite parts glow. We've even had moms buy it for their young kids. You can find this at www.holidayproducts.com.

One of the most popular bath gels and after shower sprays is Classic Erotica's Body Dew Shower Gel and After Bath Mist with Pheromones. They are both popular at Lady Bliss home parties. They are affordable and smell heavenly. Also available are samplers for both the gel and the oil, which make great gifts and giveaways. You can buy all these at www.holidayproducts.com.

Always a favorite at Lady Bliss home parties is Coochy Shave Cream. It's made to help eliminate any razor rash after you shave your bikini line, as well as make the experience much more comfy. Women also use this on their legs and we have heard of men who use it on their face to help with razor burn. You can find this at www.holidayproducts.com.

Spray Talcs for Bed and Body

These are found in most sex-toy party kits. These powders are sprayed onto your sheets to impart a delightful scent and give them a powdery softness. They can also be sprayed directly onto your body, which is especially nice on a hot summer day. Some sprays are enhanced with pheromones to really "raise the temperature" beneath the sheets.

One popular product that is a must-add to your kit is Classic Erotica's Silky Sheets. You can either spray it on your sheets so they smell heavenly or spray it on your skin. It is also made with pheromones to get you both in the mood. It comes in a variety of scents, but we have to confess that pear blossom is our favorite. You can find this at www.holidayproducts.com.

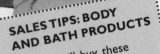

Pheromones Fragrances

These fragrances are formulated with the special chemicals, called pheromones, which our bodies produce to attract the opposite sex. These sell well at home parties because they are not too expensive and everyone wants to be sexier and more attractive to their lovers (or potential lovers). At Lady Bliss home parties we have been repeatedly told that pheromones truly work wonders. Pheromone fragrances usually have special formulations for men and for women, but a few are unisex.

SALES TIPS: BODY AND BATH PRODUCTS

Women will buy these types of products if they smell good. Pheromone-scented products have the added selling point of enhancing the libido and attracting the opposite sex. Tell single gals these products will help attract that special someone. Tell married women that they can help rekindle sexual sparks.

You will find Pure Instincts Pheromone sex attractant cologne in about every sex-toy party kit around. You just put a little on and watch what happens. The women at our parties swear by this stuff. It's available through Entrenue at 800-368-7268.

SEVENTEEN

Sexual Enhancers

exual enhancers are specially made to stimulate male and female genitalia. Some are edible, some are not. Male enhancers work wonders to help the man last longer, while achieving a more intense orgasm. Enhancers for women make the clitoris highly sensitive, to encourage a much stronger orgasmic experience. These magic potions can be numbing, cooling or warming. Women's enhancers tend to provide a tingling, warm sensation that stimulates and sensitizes the clit. Men's enhancers usually numb the penis or provide a tingling sensation. Sexual enhancers are especially helpful for men who ejaculate prematurely, and for women who have a hard time reaching orgasm.

Note: Non-edible sexual enhancers are usually made with oils that are not condom compatible. It is important to warn the women at your parties about this, in case they are using condoms for birth control or safer sex.

Nipple creams are edible, tingly sexual enhancers that make the nipples more sensitive. Nipples can be the most sen-

sitive of women's erogenous zones other than the clitoris, but for some women who have nursed children, the feeling is lost. These products are wonderful because you can actually feel your nipples again—and they are edible, which makes the experience that much more enjoyable for you and your lover!

And last but by no means least, there are products that can make you feel tighter—or as we affectionately like to say, "like a virgin again!" These creams dry up excess fluids inside the vagina and slightly swell the tissue, which helps cause more friction and give the feel of a tighter fit. They are great for women who've given birth, or are naturally very juicy.

We love the Happy Penis Cream for men—and not just for its name. For those of us who like penises, a happy one is much preferred over an unhappy one! Happy Penis Cream is edible and will numb the back of your throat to make deep oral sex easier. It comes in sampler sizes as well, perfect for gifts and giveaways. You can find it at www.holidayproducts.com.

Cleopatra Secret Cream is one of our top sellers, and will make every woman feel like a queen. It helps to make your orgasms much stronger—you might think it couldn't get any better than that, but it does: the cream is edible, so it entices him to worship you with oral pleasure. Yummy! Available through www.holidayproducts.com.

SALES TIPS: SEXUAL ENHANCERS

Explaining with humor how these products work sells them every time. For instance, when we talk about the Cleopatra Secret Cream we do it like this: "Imagine that he puts this on your sweet spot and you can start to feel yourself getting warm, but wait! It's also edible so he can go down on you too and it tastes delicious to him, which is always a plus when you want him down there longer. As it starts to make his tongue feel tingly you can tell that he's really getting into it, and it could end up being a longer more pleasurable evening than you first anticipated. Gals, isn't that always the goal?" If you put it into terms like this, you can see your customers' eyes start to fill with possibilities and they want to buy the stuff right away!

Rocket Balm is a male sexual enhancer that will make him shoot to the moon. You rub it on and it makes him tingle all over. They also carry Flower Balm for women, which helps make her feel really good too. Beware though…these products are not condom compatible and you need to make sure you tell your customers that. You can find this at Entrenue at 800-368-7268.

For nipples, Nipple Nibbler is the best. It comes in delicious flavors (our favorite is raspberry), and makes you experience your nipples in a whole new way, especially if you have not felt them in a while! You can also purchase samplers for giveaways and party gifts. You can find Nipple Nibblers at Entrenue at 800-368-7268.

Hold Tight is a product we describe as helping you feel like that virgin you once were. You just put a tiny drop on your finger right before intercourse and when it starts to tingle you know it's time to mingle! You can buy it through Entrenue at 800-368-7268.

EIGHTEEN

Sexy Accessories

We have gone over the basic product categories that will make up your main party kit, whether it's one you put together yourself or one you purchase from an established company. What follows are extras you may want to consider when you are looking to expand your offerings. They might offer your customers "how to" tips, or help them make a night of passion a little bit naughty. "Accessories" like books, videos, lingerie or light bondage products will help accentuate your sales and expand your customers' horizons.

Books

You can't beat a book for learning how to be a better lover. They can teach you new sexual positions, sex games, massage techniques, the Kama Sutra, tantric sex, how to surprise each other with erotic role-playing and more. There is also erotica written especially for couples. Reading erotica—alone or together out loud—is a wonderful aphrodisiac to help get your fantasies rolling for a terrific night in bed. Books are a useful product to carry in your sales kit, because everyone is interested in being a better lover.

Lady Bliss carries *101 Nights of Great Sex* by Laura Corn, which is a top seller. It has sealed pages that you and your lover select for a night of fun. You unseal the pages, read the erotic ad-

venture described, and then enact it. It is filled with some tame and many wild relationship-building adventures. You can find this at Entrenue at 800-368-7268.

One of our favorite books is *The Wild Guide to Sex and Loving* by Siobhan Kelly. This book gives readers all kinds of new ideas on how to spice up their sex life. It shows new po- sitions you can try with your partner, complete with tasteful pictures. We give this book two thumbs up! You can purchase this book at Entrenue at 800-368-7268.

For lovers of food (especially food that makes you want to do naughty things) we recommend *Intercourses: An Aphrodisiac Cookbook* by Martha Hopkins and Randall Lockridge. What a book! It features delicious and fabulous recipes, along with some of the most beautifully-photographed erotic images we have ever seen. This is a keeper. You can buy this book through Entrenue at 800-368-7268.

SALES TIPS: BOOKS AND VIDEOS
We all wish we knew everything there is to know about giving and receiving sexual pleasure, but when we don't, what better way to learn than by watching instructional or erotic videos or by reading great books. All of these products we've listed will add a whole new dimension to your lovemaking. Explain what the videos and books cover. If your customer has limited funds, chances are that a book or video will win out over other products if she is in the market for them.

Lingerie

At Lady Bliss we don't carry lingerie in our kits because like the rest of the fashion industry, lingerie manufacturers replace many of their lines with something new every season. For a rep, keeping up with this turnover can become expensive, let alone trying to carry different sizes, which adds to inventory costs. Our advice would be to carry sexy crotchless panties in your kit because these are almost always in stock and the styles pretty much stay the same.

We do carry lingerie on the website and we buy much of our lingerie from a company called Elegant Moments. The reason we like this manufacturer is that they don't have minimum buys and they drop-ship orders when we need them. This means we don't have to carry expensive inventory in our warehouse. However, shipping can

end up being expensive. You must keep that in the back or your mind when you are pricing your items, unless you can find a lingerie manufacturer that's close to where you do business. You can find them at www.elegantmomentslingerie.com or 800-876-4363.

Dreamgirl is another good source for lingerie. They have certain items that they always carry in stock, which helps with the problem of discontinued items. They drop-ship as well, which helps control inventory costs, and they don't have a minimum buy either. You can find them at www.dreamgirldirect.com or 800-622-5686.

Playboy has some cute leather panties and panty sets that come in nice soft pastel colors and of course in black. They do, however, have a minimum order of $100. You can find them at www.playboyleather.com or 213-747-5700.

SALES TIPS: LINGERIE

Lingerie is a gift that women can give to themselves or their partners (or their partners can give to them). It is great as foreplay to a night of lovemaking. Lingerie is also a fun way for women to indulge themselves with "a little something special just for me." Lingerie may be a safe buy for women who are attending their first home party or who feel intimidated by more sexual products.

Videos and DVDs

We suggest that you watch a video or DVD before carrying it in your party kit, so you are truly comfortable with what you are selling and can give women a realistic sense of what they will get. There are plenty of hardcore movies out there that probably won't appeal to your market, so it's better to be safe than sorry. At Lady Bliss we have a strict policy of offering only quality educational videos or erotic videos made with couples' pleasure in mind.

We have great success with Nina Hartley's how-to videos and DVDs, which teach oral sex, light bondage and more. What we love about these movies is that they have lots of sex, which men (and many women) love to watch, but they also teach you how to do something better. Nina has a strong conviction for her talents and that really comes across in her movies. You can find these at Entrenue 800-368-7268.

We also carry Candida Royalle videos and DVDs, which are made specifically for women, feature real people and have a creative story line—unlike some of the videos you buy today that are cut and re-cut to make a really bad movie. One of our favorites is called "The Gift." It's very soft: there is sex, but it's romantic and sweet. To purchase call Entrenue 800-368-7268.

Cameron Grant produces some of the most expensive adult films ever made. We just recently began carrying his movies, which are well produced and filmed in beautiful locations with beautiful people. The only thing to watch out for however, is that they are much more pornographic than a Candida Royalle movie, so our advice is to watch one of Grant's films first to see if it fits the tastes of your market. You can find these movies at Entrenue at 800-368-7268.

Light Bondage and Domination

Light bondage can be very erotic if it is consensual and done in a safe, nurturing environment. It's a great way to build trust in a relationship, while adding a whole new dimension to your usual routine. There are many products out there that offer soft approaches to this form of foreplay: satin masks to put over the eyes, furry restraints that make tie-me-up luxurious, faux fur paddles for gentle spanking, feathers to stroke and tickle the body. If presented properly and explained correctly, these products have the power to introduce your customer to a whole new realm of ecstasy.

Most sex-toy party companies carry at least one pair of handcuffs. Fantasy Lady carries a large selection of light bondage goodies.

Sportsheets has some of the sexiest light bondage kits you can find. One of our favorite kits is called Hide Your Vibe Pillow Bundle. It comes with a blindfold, cuffs, feather tickler and a little rubber whip, hidden inside a matching pillow with a secret compartment to hold all your goodies. You can find this at www.sportsheets.com.

Cathy's Cuffs has been around for over twenty years and makes some of the finest restraining kits on the market. One of the best restraint packs they sell, in our opinion, is Cathy's Deluxe Fan-

SALES ADVICE: B&D ACCESSORIES

Painting erotic scenarios is the way to sell light bondage products. Take your customers through several romantic or sexy scenes that could be accomplished with blindfolds, feathers or fur-lined handcuffs. The more daring in the group will be the ones to buy.

tasy Pak. It comes with four velvet-like restraints, a blindfold and a whip to make things interesting. To purchase go to www.cathyscuffs.com.

One of our all-time favorite bondage kits is called the 5-Piece Love Bondage Kit by Foxtails. It comes with a comfortable padded blindfold and arm and ankle cuffs. What makes this set so unique is that it's furry and comfortable, which also makes it a little less intimidating if you want to experiment with this type of sexual play. You can find this at Entrenue 800-368-7268.

NINETEEN

Manufacturers & Distributors

O ur favorite manufactures and distributors have made building Lady Bliss a joy. These companies have spent their time helping us provide our customers with the best products possible. This is why we want to reiterate how important it is to build relationships with your manufacturers and distributors. They ultimately become part of your team, a "partner" in some respects. If you need something right away, these are the folks who make sure you get it; when new products that will benefit your business have come out, they are the ones who will pass on that important information and even at times give you free samples to try out on your clientele. We even have a distributor that has passed out our information to their potential customers just because they loved our company and wanted to be part of our success. Again, we couldn't run Lady Bliss without them, and they may be able to help you as well.

Manufacturers

Top Cat-American Latex Corporation

21230 Lassen Street

Chatsworth, CA 91311

818-709-8844

www.americanlatex.com

This company provides most of the toys we carry at Lady Bliss. Not only do they have wonderful products, but they have wonderful packaging too—so important in this business.

Lover's Choice/Hot Pants

711 South Carson, Suite 4

Carson City, NV 89701

866-890-9993

www.loverschoice.tv

This company makes some of the most beautiful couples' romance kits on the market today. They are also very helpful and a pleasure to work with.

Trimensa Corporation-Forplay Lubricants

1050 Lawrence Drive

Newbury Park, CA 91320

800-554-1313

www.forplay.com

This company makes the most delicious tasty lubes you can find, and their staff is friendly and helpful.

Pulse Products-Ceduxion Products
16310 Garfield Avenue
Paramount, CA 90723-4806
562-272-4000
www.ceduxion.com

Pulse Products makes special soy candles, tasty body butters, and other body products.

Distributors

Entrenue
2681-151st Place NE
Redmond, WA 98052
800-368-7268

Entrenue provides a high-quality and varied product line that is geared towards the women's/couples market. They were very helpful to Lady Bliss when we first started, spending hours on the phone, helping us to pick out the best product line for Lady Bliss customers. They're still one of our favorite "partners."

Holiday Products
20950 Lassen Street
Chatsworth, CA 91311
800-266-5969
www.holidayproducts.com

Holiday Products also provides an excellent product line that is geared towards the women's/couples market, and we love working with them. They offer tantalizing body products under their signature line of Classic Erotica products.

B. Cumming Company

9990 Glenoaks Boulevard

Sun Valley, CA 91352

800-226-6464

B Cummings is the perfect place to purchase all of your lubricants. B Cummings is also a wonderful company to work with, a true Lady Bliss "partner."

Index

Other Ulysses Press Books

THE LITTLE BIT NAUGHTY BOOK OF SEX
Dr. Jean Rogiere, $9.95
A handy pocket hardcover that is a fun, full-on guide to enjoying great sex.

THE LITTLE BIT NAUGHTY BOOK OF SEX POSITIONS
Siobhan Kelly, $9.95
Bored with the missionary position and in need of inspiration? Fully illustrated with 50 tastefully explicit color photos, *The Little Bit Naughty Book of Sex Positions* provides everything readers need to start using these thrilling new positions tonight.

**THE SEXY BITCH'S BOOK OF DOING IT,
GETTING IT AND GIVING IT**
Flic Everett, $9.95
Offering up a snappy, smart and sassy approach to sex in the 21st century, this book dishes the dirty truth on everything from foreplay and oral sex to sex toys and fantasy games.

THE WILD GUIDE TO SEX AND LOVING
Siobhan Kelly, $16.95
Packed with practical, frank and sometimes downright dirty tips on how to hone your bedroom skills, this handbook tells you everything you need to know to unlock the secrets of truly tantalizing sensual play.

To order these books call 800-377-2542 or 510-601-8301, fax 510-601-8307, e-mail ulysses@ulyssespress.com, or write to Ulysses Press, P.O. Box 3440, Berkeley, CA 94703. All retail orders are shipped free of charge. California residents must include sales tax. Allow two to three weeks for delivery.